A NATION ONCE UNDER GOD

Christianity versus Secular Humanism
The Ultimate Struggle of our Time

Josef Herz

ISBN 978-1-64468-851-9 (Paperback)
ISBN 978-1-64468-852-6 (Digital)

Copyright © 2021 Josef Herz
All rights reserved
First Edition

All rights reserved. No part of this publication may be reproduced, distributed, or transmitted in any form or by any means, including photocopying, recording, or other electronic or mechanical methods without the prior written permission of the publisher. For permission requests, solicit the publisher via the address below.

Covenant Books, Inc.
11661 Hwy 707
Murrells Inlet, SC 29576
www.covenantbooks.com

Contents

Foreword 5

Chapter 1: The Postmodern Culture 7
Chapter 2: The Effects of the Theory of Evolution in
            the American School System 12
Chapter 3: The Decline of the Mainline Churches 15
Chapter 4: Forward to the Present Time 25
Chapter 5: How Can the Millennial Generation Be
            Blamed for This Situation? 35
Chapter 6: How Did the Early Christians Worship? 37
Chapter 7: Struggles 42
Chapter 8: What Is the Reason for Low Church Attendance? 49
Chapter 9: Islam Versus Christianity 52
Chapter 10: Redistribution of Resources 55
Chapter 11: What Kind of World Would the Millennial
            Generation Want to Leave for Their
            Children and Grandchildren? 59
Chapter 12: The Modern Family 62
Chapter 13: The Critical Importance of Christianity to
            Western Culture? 67
Chapter 14: Question: Why Would a Highly Developed
            Western University Demonize Christianity? 68
Chapter 15: One Might Ask 70
Chapter 16: The Polarization of America 79
Chapter 17: Global Climate Change 92
Chapter 18: Legal Immigration 100
Chapter 19: Political Correctness 103
Chapter 20: Christian Unity 106
Chapter 21: World Religions 110

Chapter 22: Darwinism, Marxism, Socialism 113
Chapter 23: The Power of Faith 118
Chapter 24: Economic Impoverishment through
            the Exportation of Employment
            Opportunities to Third World Countries 128
Chapter 25: Christian Morals and Values 131
Chapter 26: One Nation under God 140

Notes 141

Foreword

As a newlywed couple, we immigrated from Germany to New York City in 1963 with the hope of finding the promised land, whose streets are paved with gold, and which was somehow purveyed on German television, lip-synched in German on the only TV station in Germany at the time. *The Donna Reed Show* or *Father Knows Best* had us believing that every family in America was living in a home with a picket fence and two cars in the driveway.

Arriving in New York at night after a twelve-day journey over the Atlantic, disembarking from the ocean liner *SS Massdam* near 23rd street in Manhattan on Pier 40, Donna Reed was nowhere in sight. Nevertheless, America was for us the promised land, and we were never disappointed. It became for my wife and me the land of opportunity. Through the opportunities available, hard work, and frugal German living, the American Dream materialized and became for us a reality.

In the time span of four years, we were able to purchase that house in the suburbs and park two cars in the driveway. Purchasing a partnership share in a food-processing company ten years later, I successfully operated the company for twenty-seven years until retirement and began a new chapter in my life. Our love for the USA has prompted my wife and me to grow, not just professionally but also intellectually and spiritually. Volunteering in homeless ministry, prison ministry, geriatric pastoral, and hospital pastoral care was made possible only through the intervention and guidance of the Holy Spirit.

This book is a culmination of observations of a diminishing quality of life that has infiltrated the American culture, especially for young families just starting out.

These words are my observations about the stress and struggles families are facing now, compared to the time my wife and I arrived and started our married life together in America. The decline of a Christian worldview is of great concern to me, as I am witnessing the consequences firsthand in prisons and detox mental hospitals. TV shows with foul language and violence, and family breakups not seen or heard in a not-so-distant past, has resulted in untold suffering for families. My sincere care for the Millennial and Z Generation leads to the concern of what kind of culture will be in store for their children and their grandchildren.

A world without a Christian compass, ethics, or morals will ultimately descend into a life of anarchy and lawlessness as described in Genesis chapter 6, before the Flood, and chapter 18:20, causing the destruction of Sodom and Gomorrah and repeated numerous times throughout human history. With the nuclear capability available for the destruction of mankind in a flash, the hand of God might not even be necessary to accomplish this feat.

Josef Herz
July 20, 2019

Chapter 1

The Postmodern Culture

The Dilemma of Being a Practicing Christian in a Postmodern Secular Society

Sunday mornings across the country, children and their parents are hurrying to their church of choice. Upon entering the sanctuary as quietly as possible, not to cause too much of a disturbance, they seek a pew—maybe in the back row somewhere for a quick exit if necessary—and are finally seated. Halfway through the morning worship, one of the ministers or CE leaders will challenge the children with a biblical or Christian story. I admit, this is and has been for me one of my greatest joys, seeing the children running up to the pulpit and sitting on the floor, looking expectantly at the person presenting the story. Afterward, the parents or one of the CE board members will march them to the Christian education classrooms. The numbers have in recent years been less, but I do remember thirty years ago, in our small congregation, that twenty to thirty children were enrolled. The dedication of the Sunday school teachers has always amazed me, Sunday after Sunday, preparing for the class curriculum, praying over their students, and using their talents to the best of their ability to plant the seeds and embed Christian values into their young minds. The sheer love and energy displayed by the parents and children has compelled me to contribute to and subsidize the Christian Education Board.

Being aware of the separation of church and state here in the US and the absence of Christian education in public schools nationwide, it is an absolute necessity to educate children in the Christian faith, and hopefully when they become adults, they will become active members in a Christian church.

Looking back to the years when I was their age living in Germany, Christian education was part of public-school curriculum, and so was church attendance. The whole public-school class was marched to the nearest church, and Mass was part of our schooling one day of the week. Sunday church attendance was mandated by the church and enforced by the parents, as was First Holy Communion, Confession, and Confirmation. The Christian faith was the foundation that the secular state rested upon. The union of a man and a woman in marriage was made legal by the civil authorities in the town hall and signed by the mayor. Holy matrimony was officiated by a priest celebrating Mass. You were blessed by the priest, if you and your bride where Catholic, or by a pastor if Lutheran.

American Baptist or other nondenominational congregations were, to my knowledge, not part of the general public's belief system, as it was overwhelmingly a Catholic and Lutheran Country. Cohabitation was unlawful and frowned upon; it could even land the parents in prison for prostitution in Germany at the time.

Statistics tell us that, in 1950, the divorce rate was 5 percent, and the present rate is 50 percent, mainly due to the introduction of the no-fault divorce law. The no-fault divorce was legalized in California in 1969 and was adopted by many states soon thereafter. An increasing number of children are now growing up in a one-parent home, making it more difficult for the remaining parent to bring the children to church and to participate in activities due to their increased work schedules.

The elimination of blue laws allowed Sunday store openings, making it possible for many parents to work and earn enough to provide for the family. Two incomes are needed for a family of four to enjoy a standard of living that a single-income household was once able to provide. In 1970, the average wage of a blue-collar worker was enough to make a mortgage payment and a car payment while still being able to feed and clothe a family of four. Forward to 2018, due to the changing corporate culture, it may not be too far-fetched to believe that it requires two and a half paychecks to stay ahead of foreclosure on a house, and this while the family is living paycheck to paycheck. If day care is necessary, for lack of grandparents available to babysit part of the week, it further erodes financial stability.

When I see young families, I think, *That mom is still the heart and soul of the family and she has an incredible schedule and tasks to master to care and support her family.* The saving grace is that the husbands are more in this together with their wives and are cooperative in doing household chores than when I was a young father. Many things where never done by the husband in Germany where I grew up, which is also not so anymore. Now, moms and dads get up very early in the morning to get the children up, dressed, breakfast prepared, their own needs attended to. The husband may or may not be there due to greater travel time to work, which may be an hour or two away.

The stress level alone of a two-working-parent household is severely limiting the attendance and volunteering in their local church, as they barely have enough energy for all their family activities.

My purpose in writing this book is to make people aware of why and how this scenario had come about. When I bring up the subject of the American banking system, and how it was structured fifty years ago as family-friendly, you might be thinking, *a bank, family-friendly; yes, they really did operate under that system.*

My wife and I arrived in New York from Germany in 1963, desiring and dreaming to have a piece of the American pie. Fortunately, I found instant employment due to my training in Germany as a sausage maker, very much in demand in New York City at that time. The pay was adequate to support my wife and one son living in an apartment in the Bronx. Soon, we were able to afford a used 1958 Ford Galaxy we purchased for four hundred dollars, so we could go on weekend trips exploring the beautiful State of New York or drive to Connecticut visiting friends. After many journeys to Connecticut, we decided in 1965 to relocate there.

Moving into an apartment in Hartford and working for a beef company made it possible for us to dream about a home in the suburbs and live like the families on the *Donna Reed* or *Father Knows Best*

TV shows. We would spend our free time scouting and scouring the immediate areas around Hartford, CT, for newly developing subdivisions, where model homes where open on Sundays.

Working extra hours at my job, saving as much as possible from one paycheck, within one year we had saved enough money that we thought was enough for a down payment. I applied to every bank that would hand me an application, and soon I found one that would consider giving me a mortgage, with one provision: a 30 percent down payment, because I was an immigrant. Well, I kind of regrouped and asked my employer if he would consider allowing me to work more overtime so I would be eligible for the mortgage. He offered to lend me the $16,500.00 to purchase that house, but, not wanting to be indebted to the company, I opted for the overtime.

In 1963, American banks where family-oriented or -minded, approving mortgage money to a family only if one weekly paycheck would cover the monthly mortgage. They reasoned that a 25 percentage mortgage obligation would allow the family to be able to spend time together. Remember, in those days Sundays were still off limits for stores to be open; Sunday was a time for family gatherings. Forward to 1974, this policy was abandoned for a higher profit for the banks, the builders, and the real estate industry. With full approval of US government agencies like FHA or VA, who were regulating the housing industry, the rate to attain a mortgage was raised to 35 percent and was allowed to be based on two incomes.

Consequently, the price of the average three-bedroom house increased amazingly to 90,000 from 35,000 within the span of five years, not because the house was now bigger, but because it made more home-seekers eligible to qualify for a larger mortgage. It was celebrated as the best invention since sliced bread. And since there is a larger percentage of profit in building larger houses, small three-bedroom houses that would have qualified for GI loans were not being built anymore. Many one-income families became two-income families, and with the ingenuity of subprime mortgages, it was even possible for families to purchase a mansion with a small down payment and low initial mortgage payments that would turn into a ballooning payment within a couple of years, which most homeowners were not able to pay. It was only a matter of time when the house of cards would collapse, and it did so in 2008, with catastrophic consequences.

The flooding of the market with foreclosed houses depressed the prices below the equities of the house and subsequently slid into what are known as underwater mortgages. Families where exposed to enormous pressures from the economic situation, and in many cases, suffering the loss of their homes. The emphasis changed from maintaining a stable family environment to an enrichment of the Wall Street home mortgage manipulators (subprime mortgages), with US government regulators in full knowledge of the consequences, that these regulations will reap enormous profits for banks, but bankrupt American families.

You could easily make the comparison to the evolutionary theory of the big fish eating the small fish, and they did this with government approval. Three generations of Americans were, at that time, already schooled in evolutionary teachings and followed their inclination to get a chance to enrich themselves and possibly live in a plush larger home. The Clinton administration and the federal reserve under Alan Greenspan were repeatedly warned of the dangers of this policy and the consequences. The ballooning prime mortgages brought the world's monetary system to a catastrophic precipice as the largest banking house, Lehman Brothers, collapsed.

Chapter 2

The Effects of the Theory of Evolution in the American School System

Evolutionary teaching was adopted in the American school system in 1925, first in Tennessee, and by 1950, was mandated in all states and in all American public-school systems. Now, consider this: It boggles my mind that, fifty years ago, the American public, when polled, believed in the existence and of a Creator God; 85–90 percent believed God is the Creator and Giver of Life. Church attendance was at an all-time high, the traditional two-parent family was still intact, and the divorce rate was around 5 percent.

After evolutionary theory was introduced into the curriculum, causing me to question, how could these two teachings—one, we are created by God; and the other, we are direct descendants of apes—correlate; and how is it possible for children to understand and live with two drastically different teachings side by side in all their years in public schools? A child is brought to church on Sunday or Bible study during the week for an hour or two, and spends five days, thirty hours, in an environment where even prayer and the mention of a Creator is punishable by law. Town-sponsored sports competitions are scheduled on Sunday mornings, at the same time when Sunday worship is conducted. A parent, not wanting to deprive their children of those activities, is not able to attend church either.

So when I see beautiful, bright-eyed children every Sunday morning all excited running to their Sunday school classrooms, I think, how could these children not suffer an identity crisis when, on

Monday, they are in a public school and are taught by their teacher that their ancestors were apes? And who is really sure what kind of an ape? A baboon or a gorilla? I have no knowledge of any kind of ethical laws or morals these beautiful creatures live by or adhere to.

If God in heaven is not our creator as the children are taught, and that they are not a child of God created in his image, and what the Bible teaches is irrelevant and not true anymore, one can only wonder, how could a child know what is truth? It has been amply demonstrated by not just a few dictatorial governments in Europe, Asia, and South America how the evolutionary doctrine was applied to the general population. The American eugenics movement justified the limiting of the black population by legalized sterilization.

I want to address the Millennial generation (1981-2010) who are a direct product of this secular-modern teaching, where absolutes do not exist and each person can decide what moral laws to follow and their lifestyles are a matter of choice and personal preference. A correction officer escorted me out of a youth detention facility and made a comment that struck me. Aware that I was conducting Bible studies for the inmates, he commented, "It is good that you teach about a god, but it does not matter what someone believes as long as it works out for them." Which means that I decide, and not moral laws that apply to my life. Laws are in danger of not being respected, because who on this earth has the right to tell me how and with who I want to have a relationship with.

They themselves want to decide in what combination their living arrangements shall be and how they want to live their lives. I have ministered in youth correctional facilities for the last twenty-five years as a chaplain volunteer, to young men between of the ages of fifteen to twenty-one. The majority of them were growing up in a single-parent household, many without their father or any father figure in their lives, many being raised by their grandparents, who were elderly and unable to control their grandchildren, who spend much of their time on the streets.

The grandparents do their utmost best, but in many cases are not successful in teaching moral values and ethics, because the neighborhood rule of law is what the street dictates. I have been involved in this ministry, not strictly for religious reasons, but being 100 percent sure the only real chance of survival for these children is faith in God, and lacking that, they become prey to whatsoever the current trend the culture glorifies; and sadly, in recent years, it has been the gun-and-drug culture. Too many lose their precious young lives to overdoses and gunshot wounds, not only from police but their own peers and neighbors. To me, all young men are precious children of God, and God has a plan for every one of his children.

I am not so sure if the governing bodies and agencies in charge have their best welfare at heart. Forgive me, but if they all would turn their lives around and not continue a life of crime, how many people working for the prison system, would be able to earn the kind of salaries and benefits state employees enjoy? I have been told by a senior retired correctional official that the recidivism rate of the offenders attending Christian programs are well below secular programs. No wonder that in many instances our Christian chaplain volunteers have encountered many instances where entry was not possible because of mysterious disappearances of the lists of offenders required before entering or the volunteer admittance approvals could not be found.

Chapter 3

The Decline of the Mainline Churches

Can we really point fingers at the younger generation? After all, they did not create this ideology of postmodernism with no absolutes and no restrictions on their preferred lifestyles that is so prevalent in our culture. Churches by and large continue as they always have operated. Most of their resources and energies are consumed by the maintenance of the building, salaries, and operating costs. There are more Bible studies and books and materials available for spiritual growth than any other time in history. I hate to make the comparison of a college student who studies most of his life without applying his knowledge in his adult life and able to show any tangible results. There is obviously a need to study the Scriptures; it is a living document and it provides a road map for living a life worth living in this world. But as the Lord told the Pharisees, "You diligently study the Scriptures, because you think that by them you possess eternal life" (John 5:39). The Word is more powerful than a two-edged sword and, if shared and lived, is a powerful weapon that worldly powers cannot overcome.

What comes to my mind are the dictators and rulers throughout history have in every instance made the reading of the Bible a major offense, in some places even punishable by death. Why? Because they know it is very powerful and dangerous weapon in the hands of common folks, more powerful than a two-edged sword. It begs the question: how could these avowed atheist dictators and rulers know this, and why those very learned in Scripture not using this weapon against them?

Isaiah 54:17 says, "No weapon that is formed against thee shall prosper; and every tongue that shall rise against thee in judgment thou shalt condemn. This is the heritage of the servants of the Lord, and their righteousness is from me, saith the Lord."

Martin Luther wrote the beloved hymn of the Protestant world, "A Mighty Fortress Is Our God" (translated in German as "Eine Feste Burg ist Unser Gott"). Consider the verse: "If my God is with me, who can be against me?" The battle is not fought in a church building. It is as Mother Teresa of Calcutta wrote: "We cannot save the whole world, but we can save one by one." To accomplish what Teresa said, there needs to be an army of believers reaching out right here, in our immediate neighborhoods and communities. The inner cities are drowning in desperation, and a generation of their young adults are killing or getting killed in unimaginable numbers in the last couple of years, and it doesn't look like it's abating.

The battle is on the streets of every major city in America. Inner-city churches are staffed and led by ministers and laypeople who are very dedicated but are completely overwhelmed by the secular media, which is indoctrinating the populace with the secular worldview twenty-four/seven. African American and Pentecostal churches are evident in many locations in inner cities and are great at sharing the Good News, but they are fighting a losing battle out on the street, which are controlled by drug lords and gangs. It would require someone like David Wilkerson, who wrote *The Cross and the Switchblade* to tackle the gangs of big city slums.

I would like to mention a young Englishwoman named Jackie Pullinger, who ministered in the city of Hong Kong for thirty-five years, in the district of Kowloon, which was so heroin-infested and where prostitution and crime were so rampant that the English authorities abandoned the borough and fenced it in and closed it off. Jackie was completely undeterred and unfazed; she confronted the leaders of the gangs and enlisted many of them in the fight to restore dignity and safety to the people who lived there. She fought a very difficult battle to win over the leaders of the gangs, lead many to turn their lives over to Christ Jesus, and ultimately save hundreds and thousands from a life of prostitution and drugs. Many who gave their lives to Christ escaped the horrid conditions; many former gang members came to rescue their former members.

Question: Are we willing to fence in our inner cities, casting the people off, similar what the British did in Hong Kong? One thing we need to realize is that Millennials and Generation Z, will have to live and deal with their welfare. As I mentioned before, I have not abandoned my church, but I am serving outside the church, reaching those who need a touch from Jesus. The church I support and attend is a Bible-based community; many members are generous and eager to serve the church. What I am missing is the mentoring of parishioners to step out of the box and serve in the community, especially in homeless shelters and soup kitchens.

Bible studies are an integral part of a vibrant church and provide the knowledge and undergirding for a solid foundation for the Christian to grow. There are myriad opportunities for Christians to give of themselves, their time and their energy to reach out to the homeless, whether on the streets of New York or in their own communities, on any given night, there are thousands of people living on the streets and millions are served in soup kitchens every day of the week. I have personally led groups to New York and local ministries, and encouraged people I met in parishes to take that step of faith and be involved, and in every instance, it has opened their hearts and minds to the need of their less fortunate neighbors. The mission of a church is to mentor and equip their congregants to become the hand and feet of Jesus on this earth. In too many cases, a church will deteriorate into a building maintenance organization, or into a country club atmosphere where it is more important, who you worship with, than who we are there to worship.

The dynamic to serve outside the church has evaporated in recent years, to the point that maintaining the organization and the upkeep of the building are now the main mission of the church. Many churches are resembling a country club, where the maintenance of the golf course and the upkeep of the clubhouse are central, and networking among the members with influence and wealth and can prove very beneficial for their career advancement. This has led to lukewarm churches that are coasting along, as I would describe it; there is no more urgency to equip the faithful in the mission that Mother Teresa was talking about. Why step out of this beautiful box, when there are such wonderful benefits to be had, and that all is possible for just attending the right church?

With endowments funds in the millions, there is little appetite to confront the secular culture, but, rather continue to fall in line not causing parishioners to seek another church more aligned with the postmodern secular culture. Germany is a good example. The government collects a church tax, which allows the Catholic and the Protestant church hierarchy to reside in beautiful mansions and minister in spectacular cathedrals and basilicas. But who are they preaching to? By their own admission, only 3 percent of believing Christians attend church, whereas the Islamic faith community is erecting mosques by the hundreds and are filled with believers. Can we really blame them for living their faith?

The wealth stored in church endowments and investments may be a detriment here in the US, as in Germany, as long as the salaries are paid and the lights are on and the buildings are still shining. Why not be content, why change anything?

Good news is, there are many Christians who see the difficulties their fellow humans are struggling with. They are leaving the sanctuaries and using their energies and their time to make a difference in the blighted neighborhoods in the cities, some very close to their respective churches. This may be the answer for the Millennial and Zoomer generation; they are very alert to the issues their brothers and sisters in inner cities are struggling with and would be very willing to be part of their renewal.

The starfish story comes to mind. A boy stands near the water on the beach and picks up starfish one at the time and throws them back into the water. A man comes by and tells the boy, "What are you doing? There are millions of starfish. What difference does it make to them?" The boy picks up another one, throws that one in, and says to the man, "I bet I made a difference to that one."

I heard two testimonies from two different people, in two different locations: one a young black girl, who informed me that by my assuring her of the fact that she is a child of God and loved by

God, despite all her difficulties, she is now turning to God. The other person, a white man in his late eighties who contemplated suicide after being placed in a geriatric long-term care facility. He became depressed and contemplated how to accomplish suicide. He had completely given up on life, but I had the privilege to share the love of Christ with him and visited him as much as I was able. He has now become the darling of the caretakers and nurses.

One time, as I was walking the floors in a local hospital, a man ran after me, begging me to come to the room his mother was in as a patient, and told me very emotionally how I came to see him in the maximum-security prison eight years earlier, and how he finally came to realize that he was not trash but a child of God and a conqueror in Christ Jesus. His life changed. He overcame his anger, and credited Jesus for opening his eyes to see. All this tells me that I am on the right path, not for my glory, but only for the glory of God.

In the Book of Acts, we read example after example of how average folks reached out to those around them, even sharing their belongings. Acts 2:44 says, "All the believers were together and had everything in common. They sold property and possessions to give to anyone who had need. They broke bread in their homes and ate together with glad and sincere hearts, praising God and enjoying the favor of all the people. And the Lord added to their number daily those who were being saved."

Consider that the first Christian church building ever built was located in a cave underneath the Saint George Church in the town of Rihab in northern Jordan—where it's thought early Christians fled to escape persecution. Built in AD 230, Saint George is believed to be the oldest "proper" church building in the world. For the early Christians, the church was the people, not the building. The first Christians met in people's houses. Colossians 4:15 says, "Salute the brethren which are in Laodicea, and Nymphas, and the church which is in his house." Philemon 1:2 reads, "And to our beloved Apphia and Archippus our fellow soldier, and to the church in their house." This might show us the way to reach those in our blighted immediate neighborhoods: being aware of their needs, and sharing in a family atmosphere where people may reconnect again in a house church.

Lord knows, many parishioners live in houses large enough to accommodate great numbers of people who could pray and break bread together. As the technological advances available to us today have connected and separated people of all ages, and loneliness afflicts more and more people, lives resemble more like those of hermits, now glued to their screens, be it cell phones, iPads, or a large-screen TV, one-on-one conversations are not the order of the day anymore as it was before these technological wonders became mainstays of the culture.

The power of the Gospel has never lost its strength in touching lives. The Word is still more powerful than a two-edged sword, but it must be shared in its original form. Many churches in America, large and small, have resorted to elaborate entertainments, recruiting professional-grade musicians for their praise and worship services. Many churches have invested a considerable effort of time and energy in charismatic services, whipping worshippers into a trance with endless repetition of the lyrics and decibels loud enough to be worthy of a Rock Concert. I remember one worship service we attended where the reverberation caused my insides to reverberate, to the point that we had to leave the performance halfway through. I was not sure who the attending worshippers where worshipping, the performers or the Lord. That band disbanded within a short time after that performance, the reason being that the musicians squabbled among themselves over who would control the sound volume of their musical instrument; in other words, who is able to out drown the singers and the other instruments.

Someone wrote, "The church does not exist to entertain the saved. It exists to train the saved to glorify God and reach the lost." Elaborate sound systems and sophisticated graphics on screens the size of walls, and professional musicians performing on stage repeating lyrics continuously until worshippers are in a frenzy, and in some cases, drop to the floor and writhe uncontrollably, so that one is concerned for their well-being? My wife, who suffers from epilepsy, was extremely disturbed.

TV evangelists are broadcasting nationwide; one in particular, in Texas, broadcasts from a former football stadium, filled to the brim with a weekly attendance of 52,000 worshippers and entertainment rivaling any rock concert. It serves a short prosperity message, giving people the impression that they too can name it and claim it. After all, Jesus said, "You have not, because you asked not. If you have faith as small as a mustard seed, then you can say to this mountain and move it out to sea."

The question arises: would the worshippers be better off attending small churches? Are they nourished and better able to deal with their daily struggles to survive and find the strength and hope for a better tomorrow? The pitfall of a prosperity gospel is that when reality sets in and their expectations are not met, and frustration or disappointment shows its ugly face, then where will they turn to?

The lifestyle of the TV preachers tells a more bizarre and different story, with personal net worths in the hundreds of millions; they are resembling more and more the Catholic hierarchy living in palaces and worshipping in cathedrals that are filled only on special occasions and when broadcast on TV nationwide or even worldwide.

I have, on occasion, on my visits to my hometown in Germany, attended Mass in a basilica that was build to seat 2,000 worshippers. I would look around and count the attending faithful; many mornings, they numbered more in the twenties. As of this date, even those Masses have ceased for lack of priests and lack of worshippers. The basilica is presently only used for special celebrations.

The hope and renewal may very well come from the Millennial generation. They are not as easily misled or impressed with the flowing robes and tassels as the generations before them. I think they deserve great respect for their keen, observant awareness of the financial burdens the pomp and circumstance require in financial contributions, which are not benefitting their brothers and sisters in need, who are living from paycheck to paycheck or from hand to mouth. There has been one instance that came to light, where a bishop of the diocese of Limburg, Germany, remodeled his residence, a castle, to the tune of 42 million and installed a bathtub made from pure gold. The uproar upon the revelation caused the Vatican to remove him from that diocese and reassign him to a smaller diocese. The damage from that episode caused many faithful to abandon Mass, and large numbers withdrew their contributions and are not supporting the church anymore.

Other countries also have suffered large declines in attendance and support: Ireland and South American countries come to mind. Priests' abuse of children, and in many cases, abuses by cardinals of seminarians, not turning over the offenders to the local judiciary, all come to mind. When we consider all this, is it any wonder why the folks in the pews are restless and many speak with their feet?

The question remains: where does the Christian who wants to worship go, and what will church life look like once the silver-haired worshippers are not there to support the church anymore? Perhaps the church will have to return to the original form of gathering and the sharing and breaking of the bread, just as the Amish are still celebrating the Lord's Day. This is their way of life, being mostly agrarian, which may not be feasible for the general American public, as we live overwhelmingly in large metropolitan areas and inner cities.

During the Kennedy administration, there was a new initiative called the Peace Corps, and to date there have been 187,000 Peace Corps volunteers and trainees with the average age of about twenty-eight years old. A similar initiative could be the answer for the Millennials by serving and mentoring children from kindergarten on through high school and college, and mentoring unemployed workers who do not have the skills necessary to find employment in the new digital economy where opportunities abound, and where labor shortages exists. This is almost a replay of the Great Depression, where millions of workers were unprepared for the industrial revolution that coincided with the financial collapse on Wall Street.

Retirees who are in need to bolster their funds and need motivation to start another day are finding meaning for their remaining years by volunteering or returning to the workforce, and the young who work alongside with them would most likely be the biggest beneficiaries. In my own case, I knew myself too well to leave the business world at sixty-seven and not have a purpose to wake up to and a mission to accomplish something.

I was maybe a little more ahead in this search, as the Lord has opened a myriad of doors for me where I would feel very much needed. Caring ministry in a youth prison, spiritual care in a local hospital, and conducting religious services in a mental facility, all on a volunteer basis, has become a big part of my life. Along with the learning involved in writing outlines for the messages that I share, the time and energy to commute to the places of service and the commitment necessary to be reliable, I could not imagine my life without the volunteer work. The energy and stamina at this stage in my life is sometimes a challenge; just imagine what a person in their twenties would be able to accomplish.

Realistically, yes, many have families and children, but look at the role model they would be for their own children by not spending countless hours surfing the Internet or watching football games for hours at time. There is a slogan that goes around, "Perform random acts of kindness." As a believer in Christ, why not change that to "Perform purpose-driven acts of kindness"? Every human being is provided with 168 hours a week; even one hour of the 168 a week doing a purpose-driven act of kindness, multiplied be the number people who identify themselves as Christians, could transform our nation, so we could truly announce and unabashedly say, "We are a Christian nation."

Emigrating from Germany to America fifty-five years ago, being the beneficiary of the generous American kindness and spirit, I am not aware of any other nation on earth that has donated so generously much of their wealth to other nations in their difficulties, many of them self-inflicted, but they nevertheless reached out and are still doing it. Why not be there for our own people, right here in our own cities and towns where boys and girls who are fatherless and elderly who are lonely? In my youth prison ministry, I pose this question to the young adults: "Who raised you? Did you have a mom and a dad in your upbringing?" The answer is almost universally "My grandmother." In extreme cases, both mom and dad are incarcerated.

When asked, "How did you spend your time after school was out?" without fail, the answer was "the street." Drug lords are recruiting children into their sales force, even children as young as eight to ten years old. Many years ago, I was invited to visit the Harlem neighborhood where many churches have initiated after-school mentoring programs, specifically between the time they are released from school to the time their parents were able to pick them up after work, providing lunches and mentoring with their homework.

Most of the volunteers are retired folks, business executives, policemen, factory workers—people from all walks of life. Campus Crusade for Christ was providing the guidance, and, to some degree, financial assistance. I am convinced there needs to be a redistribution of time and commitment to social causes. What I mean by that is to redirect the amount of feel-good charity work for the most part, the serving on organizational church committees, restoration of buildings built in a different era when worshipping a building and maintaining was tantamount to serving the Lord, in many cases with the understanding that it would be a guarantee for a sure passage into heaven. This model is still observed in many churches today, regardless of denomination. There was a time in history when a cathedral would be under construction for three hundred years, reaching immense heights. Artisan stonework and statues required unimaginable funds and sacrifice, exacted by the ruling class and the church hierarchy from the poor peasants, who struggled in most cases just to stay alive. This form of slavery in Germany, known as Leibeigentum, existed up until the time that it was abolished by Frederick the Great, King of Prussia (1740-86).

Chapter 4

Forward to the Present Time

2018

Megachurches are numerous, with attendance in the 15 to 30 thousands congregants weekly, many of whom are able to contribute substantial amounts to sustain the enormous structures and exorbitant salaries of the lead pastors, who in many cases own mansions and townhouses in several cities. Small storefront churches have sprung up in cities across the country, many in very depressed neighborhoods where the poverty rate is at or below the national average. Parishioners are exhorted by pastors using Holy Scripture to justify luxurious lifestyles. The parishioners contribute of their meager funds and tithe to these churches, in many of which the pastor is not even ordained by a seminary or denomination, causing legitimate recognized churches to experience financial difficulties and thereby increasing the burden on their own worshippers.

I am familiar with the situation of a church in a city of 50,000, where the founding pastor was working two jobs, never accepting any remuneration, a true man of God, faithfully teaching and mentoring his flock. This pastor reminds me of the apostle Paul working as a tanner and tentmaker to support himself so not to be a burden on the tiny congregations. The church, through the faithful and frugal administration, and from the contributions of the congregation, was debt free and growing.

Upon the pastor's retiring, a new pastor was appointed to lead the congregation. He had dreams of being the senior pastor of a megachurch, or, in this case, he was planting new churches in surrounding towns and thereby hollowing out and impoverishing the once-thriving mother church. Upon his retiring, the church was deep in debt, which left the mother church in dire circumstances, not being able to pay for the oil to heat the sanctuary. The pastor chosen to lead the congregation following the previous pastor used his personal credit card to pay for the delivery of heating oil to heat the building, enough to prevent the pipes from freezing.

Sadly, this scenario is not an isolated case. There is a proliferation of new storefront churches springing up with elaborate digital displays and messages relayed by pastors via Zoom from a distant location to the worship venue. Like pop stars in the secular world, eventually they lose their popularity and their charisma to continuously draw new worshippers. Sometimes they fall prey to the power of admiration, in some cases almost to the level of idolizing the lead pastor. They misuse the availability of funds provided by the faithful, and there is misappropriation of the collections.

It has been the case in many mega- or not-so-mega-churches that the following would find a more dynamic speaker or more elaborate and more advanced praise and worship team in another church that provides professional quality entertainment. Meeting worshippers I personally know from an earlier time, I would ask them, "Are you still in the church where we met?" and apologetically, they admit that they found something more to their liking. Some had changed the congregation they attend for worship two to three times and will give you a splendid testimony of how their spiritual need is now nourished and how it has improved their walk with the Lord.

I was once listening to a pastor speak about the local church community. He was accusing other pastors of sheep-stealing and now they are reluctant to organize events together. The constant shifting of worshippers from one congregation to another is a form of rearranging the deck on the *Titanic*.

The number of faithful is not growing, it is even declining, and because of division in the Church, they are losing the power that lies in numbers to confront the authorities who are rewriting the tenets of the Bible. Leading authorities are proclaiming instead the gospel according to TV or the desires of the dark powers, where the killing of the unborn and establishing unnatural unions are now the law of the land. Euthanasia may not be far behind, and will soon become the law, as it is already on the books in the Netherlands and Belgium. This was the struggle the Catholic Church had to deal with the last two thousand years, where kings and despots demanded the clergy to receive their theology from the present rulers and not from the bishops and popes.

This is not implying that all popes have led exemplary lives; yes, there were quite a few bad apples, but dealing with very bad rulers appointing themselves and justifying their actions by the grace of God is what eventually led to the Reformation. This is the same issue in the present culture. The court is deciding what is lawful with total disregard of what the law of God has explicitly forbidden, even to the extreme point that clergy, shop operators, and artisans are forced to perform and participate in ceremonies for fear of lawsuits that are violating their consciences and beliefs.

Houses of God, in their splintered state and divisions, are hopelessly powerless to resist this intrusion into the God-ordained natural laws and the grab for power, and since power by definition is held by the greater numbers, they are totally overwhelmed.

God has blessed the United States with a Constitution that is without equal in the modern world. The people have the power of the vote to unseat members of congress and likewise senators, but as the Lord warned us repeatedly, a divided house cannot stand. Mark 3:25 says, "And if a house is divided against itself, that house will not be able to stand." Ephesians 4:4 tells us, "There is one body and one Spirit, just as you were called to one hope when you were called; one Lord, one faith, one baptism; one God and Father of all, who is over all and through all and in all." In 1 Corinthians 8:6, we find, "Yet for us there is but one God, the Father, from whom all things came and for whom we exist. And there is but one Lord, Jesus Christ, through whom all things came and through whom we exist."

This teaching is very clear in what division does to the body of Christ, and we are witnessing the decline and the results in large numbers already. I have serious concerns regarding the participation of the younger generation in the life of the Christian churches regardless of the affiliation or denomination. This trend is not only occurring in churches but also in civic organizations and ethnic clubs, which have, in years gone by, served as networking centers for jobs and other opportunities, whether social or business. The movement is toward a digital world, communicating for the most part through social media in our nation and worldwide, using an advertisement slogan from forty years ago, "Let your fingers do the walking."

Never in my wildest imaginations could I have foreseen the event of being connected to the whole world by a little handheld device the size of a pack of cigarettes. I have seen children as young as eight years old and older adults in the sanctuary during the Mass or worship service reaching for their cell phones and texting or receiving calls and messages. Reaching into their pockets or handbags is not a sign of generosity to reach for the wallet anymore. Makes one wonder, who is leading this new behavior, the young, the old, or vice versa? And how can the gospel message be relayed and made relevant in this atmosphere of worshippers who are multitasking and fragmenting their attention? Could it be possible that there needs to be a return to the original model?

The original model means sharing the Good News on a small scale with family, friends, and colleagues, and participating in networking and meetings in houses. This may be opposed in many quarters for reasons of interfering with the hierarchical structures that denominations are built upon. Priests and pastors spent four to eight years in seminaries studying theology, and upon graduation become administrators of parishes or congregations. Studying the origin of the Christian faith and church, we find that the people who led and congregated following the Pentecost were to a large degree average people whom the Lord had touched; it was the Holy Spirit that enabled them and equipped and led the Apostles and the people of the way.

Note: The first 150 years after the resurrection, the Christian faith underwent enormous growth, so much so that it may have contributed to the persecution by the Roman authorities of the people of the Way. Crosses were not seen, except crucifixions. Followers of

Jesus were known as the people of the Way. In John 14:6, Jesus said, "I am the way and the truth and the life. No one comes to the Father except through me." If you ask people on the street at random, "How does one get into heaven?," at this point, many would answer, "Just be a good person," not acknowledging that Jesus is the sure way, not just some way.

To go a little further, many clergy are constantly proclaiming the Scripture from the Gospel of Luke 23:43: "And Jesus said unto him, Verily I say unto thee, today shalt thou be with me in paradise." Meaning it does not matter what heinous crime you have committed, if a second before your death you ask like the repenting thief on the cross, you will be, on the same day, in paradise. Since many scholars are divided about the comma, especially since the original language did not use commas, inserting the comma after *today* changes the meaning. It can also be interpreted as "I tell you the truth today, you will be with me in paradise" versus "today, you will be with me in paradise." The question arises, when and how?

Many discussions have centered around the Apostles' Creed: "Jesus was crucified, died and was buried; He descended into hell; on the third day He rose again from the dead; He ascended into heaven, and is seated at the right hand of God the Father Almighty; from there He will come to judge the living and the dead." The more I study Holy Scriptures, the more doubts arise in my mind about the concept of last-minutes salvation. Serving as a volunteer pastoral care chaplain in hospices and ICUs has made me doubt even more about the validity of the comma.

Matthew 25:31 talks about the separation of the sheep and the goats where we are judged by what we have done and what we have failed to do, but this is undermined by the passage in Ephesians 2:8, that says, "For by grace you have been saved through faith, and this is not your own doing; it is the gift of God." A gift is something we receive without any effort or payment. How this can be understood and defended in light of Matthew 7 and Matthew 25 still escapes me.

I totally understand what Jesus did on the cross has made it possible for us to be forgiven, but a gift is only a gift if we make the decision to accept the precious gift, if we ask to be forgiven and a change of life follows. John 5:28–35 (NIV) says, in part, "Do not be amazed at this, for a time is coming when all who are in their graves will hear his voice and come out—those who have done what is good will rise to live, and those who have done what is evil will rise to be condemned." I bring this up for discussion in the interest of helping to find the answer to the issue of a large numbers of young adults, whether in church or in the general population, who are not regular churchgoers but want to live a life pleasing to the Lord.

There is no government employment manual that allows the recitation of Psalm 19:14, "Let the words of my mouth, and the meditation of my heart, be acceptable in your sight, O Lord, my strength, and my redeemer." I beg you to find this in any government manual or law book. If we are not concerned about God, but only about the governing bodies, then why do we incarcerate 2.5 million lawbreakers in the US? The offenders in the majority of cases are incarcerated because they failed in their mission to defraud or murder someone without detection. Jesus made this very clear in Mark 8:36: "For what shall it profit a man, if he shall gain the whole world, and lose his own soul?" Now, the next question arises, what about those who succeeded? How likely are these people to lead other people to the Lord?

What I am driving at, is it possible to expect students of all ages and grades to consider their conscience when the official teaching material does not allow the teaching of our Lord in any public school? Augustine of Hippo wrote, "Our hearts are restless, until they find rest in you" (354–430), in his *Confessions*. When I was in my teens and experienced difficult situations, my refuge was to walk into a church and just sit very quietly in the pew and open my heart to God. I poured out my troubles and my poor state, and afterwards my focus shifted from being distressed to "I can overcome."

Comparing those times, more than sixty years ago now, to the present, the balm people use now to cope with their struggles is some form of hallucinatory drug, uppers or downers, depending on the severity of the problem the person experiences. In the absence of ethical and moral moorings or basis, the answer they seek will be the instant relief or gratification experienced by alleviating the pain for a moment. But like all sin, first it creates a barrier between the sinner and God, and as Paul points out so vividly in Romans 6:23, "The wages of sin is death." At this moment in our country, the deaths due to overdose has skyrocketed and outpaced even death by motor vehicles, cancer, and heart attacks.

The next question comes to mind: with the rate of lethal overdoses, the rate of aborted babies, the low birth rate (not as acute in the US as in other countries), and the rate of longevity, with people living approximately 15 to 20 years longer, how is it possible to support and care for the aged? Some European countries have introduced and enacted legislation that legalizes euthanasia. When the burden of caring for the afflicted becomes greater than the contribution of the rest of society, their quality of life is questioned, and, if deemed appropriate, they are euthanized.

I have yet to meet a millennial or young worshipper in a church who understands the philosophy of eugenics that was propagated by Margaret Sanger. The evolutionary teaching of the bigger fish eating the weaker smaller fish and the attempts to create a superior race have contributed to the biggest holocaust known to man.

Psalm 139:13–16 says, "For you created my inmost being; you knit me together in my mother's womb. I praise you because I am fearfully and wonderfully made; your works are wonderful; I know that full well. My frame was not hidden from you when I was made in the secret place, when I was woven together in the depths of the earth. Your eyes saw my unformed body; all the days ordained for me were written in your book before one of them came to be."

A government that enacts and enforces laws that are contrary to the teachings of God, the Creator of heaven and earth, has the Declaration of Independence, which states that man is endowed by his creator with certain inherent and inalienable rights, including the preservation of life, liberty, and the pursuit of happiness. It also says that if the people have been denied these rights, they have the right to rebel against their government.

Why have we not seen or heard of any mass demonstrations organized by the American Bible-believing churches against a government that is denying the Christian believers their right to believe the Holy Bible? The constant bombardment by the media of what constitutes political correctness, the legislative bodies enacting laws that are reflecting the lifestyles of the present culture, whether it be cohabitation, free sexual relations with no strings attached, no absolutes and no commitments, and abortion on demand. As one House representative explained, "Don't blame us, we are only giving the people what they want." So, who or where are the gatekeepers? These lifestyles are destroying the bedrock of society, a family where children can grow up in a stable and secure environment and know values that are ethical, moral, and beneficial to themselves and society.

Without a moral compass, it is not very hard to see why the Word of God is not that necessary in their lives; problem is, they may only think they can supplant God's Word and they themselves are God! How could their guidelines serve them as a guiding light and still allow them to accept Jesus's teaching, "I am the way and the truth and the life. The evil one is the father of lies, I have come to give life, the evil one only comes to kill and destroy." In Jeremiah 29:11, God says, "I have plans for you, to give hope and a future, to prosper you and not to harm you."

Example: Wolves are one of the smartest animals to survive in the harshest climate in the northern wilderness. They are team workers in their hunting techniques. They do not charge into the center of a of flock of sheep; they circle the herd until they notice one sheep that separates from the flock, which then provides them with an easy opportunity to devour that sheep. First Peter reminds us: "The evil one is like a roaring lion prowling around for an opportunity to devour us." Not being part of a Christian community, not being nourished by the Word, not living by the precepts of the Word, leaves especially the young very vulnerable to seeking their precepts and guidance from the Gospel according to TV, the very popular postmodern theology devoid of any absolutes or morals.

We are now living in a postmodern society, sans Christian morals. Gay and lesbian clergy are living as husband and wife, serving as senior pastors in mainline congregations, in many cases being active in LGBT demonstrations and educational institutions, promoting transgender acceptance. Children as young as five years old given a choice of what gender they want to grow up as, a boy or a girl! Science has proven that DNA cannot be altered in children in the development stage of their lives without serious consequences, either physical or mental suffering. How can a child digest this dichotomy and contradiction of teaching? The biblical definition: God created man and woman. The secular teaching: you can chose what you want to be. If you ask a child at the age of five what he or she wants to be when they grow up, every other week you may get a different answer. Those changes generally do not have serious consequences. The Castrati exploitation of boys for operatic purposes was a disaster and was abolished in the late 1800s, after realizing this was reason for the deforming of extremities and facial features.

This whole new philosophy contradicts what the world has understood and is accepted since the earliest scriptural writing and obviously very necessary for the procreation of the human species.

Abortion is another distortion of creation's necessity. Many nations are waking up to the reality of this fact, that without enough babies born, the future of the elder generation is in serious trouble. The present health of the social security contract is not secured when the young working generation is supporting an ever-increasing aging generation. This situation will ultimately lead to euthanasia of the elderly and justified with the explanation that they are not able to enjoy the level of a quality of life a younger person is entitled to.

What is a millennial to take away from this postmodern culture? Number one, Biblical teaching is obviously incompatible with this new reality of legally permitting the killing babies in the womb, and now in some states, after birth, euthanasia by choice (with a doctor's assistance in life-ending procedures), or family or ethic committees deciding who is eligible to access the assets of relatives or society. Without a radical shift of understanding the meaning in life, things we can change, and things that we cannot change without catastrophic consequences, what kind of world will we live in?

The universal human rights state: the basic rights and freedoms, to which all humans are entitled, include the rights to life, liberty, equality, and a fair trial, freedom from slavery and torture, and freedom of thought and expression. Those poor souls that are of college age or slightly older are now scrutinized for every word spoken, if it meets the new standard of politically correct speech, freedom of expression severely curtailed under the mantle of "hate speech." Life as previous generations understood it is not protected anymore, subject to the interpretation of a liberal set of educators and justices. How did this evolve? How did the baby boomer generation accept these destructive policies of biblical-based societal values? Especially when that generation still attended and believed in God by a large margin, maybe 80 percent all through the time when the legislative bodies and the courts enacted laws forbidding school prayers, legalizing no-fault divorces, making abortion legal, legalizing gay and lesbian marriages, forcing people of faith to pontificate and assist in these marriages, opposing views are sued and forced into bankruptcies.

Chapter 5

How Can the Millennial Generation Be Blamed for This Situation?

I think not! It seems to me, this glacial movement away from Christian moral and ethics has been in a transitional mode many years before this millennial generation has been born. The 1960 sexual revolution was just the opportunity for the apostles who proselytized unrestrained sexual practices, and the introduction of the birth control pill made this teaching even more popular and it reached the climax in Woodstock, NY. There was the popularization of cannabis and LSD, which unfortunately caused the death of many of the most talented and gifted musicians and artists of the time. I would argue that many of the Woodstock generation have in some way continued to enjoy the use of hallucinogenic drugs and relaxed many taboos even as they started families. Many baby boomers became legislators and judges who liberalized the culture they enjoyed in their heyday of no limits in their way of life. Their children observe their parents smoking cannabis at their house parties.

A new teaching of no winners or losers in a game of sports was introduced to promote a child's self-esteem; all are awarded trophies so as not to hurt anyone's feelings. Healthy competition in sports is stifled and does not prepare children for the challenges of life.

Children decide the rules of the house, and a very limited amount of discipline is demanded from their parents and in public schools. It is not hard to conclude that a Bible-teaching church is not one of their favorite activities to participate in or live by with their moralistic precepts and views. Biblical teaching and Christian morals are contrary to a free-love culture, which manifests itself in the decline of traditional marriage, the commitment required to enter into a covenantal relationship for life without an easy back-out provision. The new order of no-fault divorce makes it possible, if deemed unsatisfactory after a number of years, to head for the exit lane. This may be why a prenuptial contract is a prerequisite for either marriage or cohabitation in postmodern society.

Fortunately, there are still many who are not on board with this new mind-set and thrive and prosper in the confinements of marriage that has withstood the temptations. There are moms and dads who bring their children to Sunday school and are themselves attending church services and maintaining a Christian home. So, it is easy to paint a dark picture, but just as there are so many examples of failed lives lived without the blessing of God, there are just many examples of the opposite, couples who acknowledge and value the blessings of the Lord.

To bring the good news of Jesus Christ to those who are living in this world without Christ is now more than ever the responsibility of the average Christian to inspire and exhibit the positives of a covenantal marriage and living a life pleasing to the Lord. When the disciples questioned Jesus about divorce, he replied in Mark 10:5, "It was because your hearts were hard that Moses wrote you this law." Jesus was quoting from Genesis 2:24: "But at the beginning of creation God 'made them male and female.' For this reason a man will leave his father and mother and be united to his wife and the two will become one flesh. So, they are no longer two, but one flesh. Therefore what God has joined together, let no one separate."

Chapter 6

How Did the Early Christians Worship?

In the beginning of the Christian church, the followers were called the people of the Way. They worshipped in house churches. Just think for a moment, the present-day church is the most segregated gathering place on any given Sunday morning. This model probably would not have been beneficial to the spreading of the Way and the faith. The traditional church, with its confines resembling that of a certain neighborhood, maybe lily-white or all-black is segregating and dividing people, most certainly not bringing us together and learning from each other.

I have been involved for twenty-four years in the prison ministry, and have come to know many an inmate who was desperately seeking a more normal life, and I am convinced that we need to return to the root of Christianity, opening our homes to each other and fellowship together. The racial divide that exists in many a church, especially in private conversations, is rampant. I am sure it won't be easy, neither was it for the people of the Way; they all went out and lived with other people, not their own, in their missionary journeys.

Here in the US, at least for the most part, we speak the same language, live as one nation, and work together in shops and factories, but it will take more than attending numerous Bible studies and faithful attendance of church services and writing occasional checks to a charity of your choice to reclaim the fervor and commitment of the early church. People to people, one at a time, small gatherings of Bible-believing people, not just those belonging to my church, but preferably, someone who is not attending any church, otherwise we are just playing musical chairs or exchanging parishioners.

The division of denominations, which in many cases are power structures directed from a hierarchy that is protecting turf more than spreading the Gospel, has caused much suffering, even in individual families.

Would it be a major infraction of all who want to follow Jesus to share bread and wine, consecrated or unconsecrated, with each other across denominational lines? The bread we eat and the grape juice or wine we drink when we celebrate Holy Communion is in all surety provided by our Lord, and if we chose to believe in the actual presence of our Lord Jesus in the form of his body and his blood, and another participant believes only in his spiritual presence, or only in remembrance what the Lord did for us on that cross on Calvary, what would Jesus want us to do, separate us?

Ephesians 4:4–7 (NIV) says, "There is one body and one Spirit, just as you were called to one hope when you were called; one Lord, one faith, one baptism; one God and Father of all, who is over all and through all and in all. But to each one of us grace has been given as Christ apportioned it." This is the model that would bring all worshippers together in unity and be enriched by the diversity it would bring to our homes, which have in recent times become digital enclaves without eye-to-eye contact or personal conversation. God created us for community. It is written in Genesis: "It is not good for man to be alone; we are made for fellowship." St. Augustine again: "Lord, thou hast made us for thy self, and our hearts are restless until they rest in you."

Communication with our Lord in prayer and singing and reading his Word and fellowship with our neighbors and friends is exactly what it means to be a follower of Christ.

These gatherings would also serve as networking avenues for all the needs people are likely to have, just as in the beginning where there was the additional threat of persecution, therefore the sign of the fish, informing fellow followers of a safe house or passage. For that matter, many houses in my neighborhood display a sign in plain sight, ADT, ATT, or some other security company, warning intruders not to try to force themselves in. So, we could place some sign in front where it would be easily visible that this house is safe for Bible study and prayer. Walking around the neighborhood, like the Mormon missionaries do, and knock on many doors, why not invite seekers of the Word in and be in the presence of fellow believers?

Sadly, my wife and I have lived in our neighborhood for thirty-five years, and we have failed miserably, as we hardly know anyone living around us. The church we attend is the only connection we have to the town we live in, and even there, we have a difficult time befriending couples or people our age. Young families with small children congregate more with families in similar circumstances and similar issues they struggle with and different likes they enjoy.

One of the reasons my wife and I decided not to move into an adult-only housing community is we enjoy the sight and noise of families with small children. Whenever we are out shopping and notice how many families have two or three children in tow, which here in America is still commonplace, it is for us a sight that we enjoy. Now this shows that the demographics are still in positive territory, and the influx of immigrants, legal or illegal, gives us hope, compared with the EU, where there are serious concerns about the lack of sufficient numbers of children to maintain the social contract of young versus old. A shortage of workers, especially in the health field, and an aging population living far longer is taxing the Social Security to the point that the EU in many countries was required to extend the age of eligibility to collect social security upward to sixty-seven years and maybe even higher in the near future.

This trend brought on a desperate situation where the EU and individual members of the EU opened their borders to millions of refugees, mainly from Islamic countries, where the birth rate is substantially higher and adherence to their Islamic faith is far higher than those of Catholics or Protestants, necessitating the closure of churches and selling them to secular enterprises. European countries have experienced a steady decline of worshippers, and due to the smaller number of men who enter religious orders or become priests, it is especially true in the Catholic Church where sacramental requirements are part of the Catholic faith (Confession, Holy Communion, Communion of the Sick, and Holidays of Obligatory Mass).

In my own life, I have come to realize after many years that faith in God, receiving the nourishment and strength that is available in the Mass through Holy Communion, the readings of the Gospels, and the practice of prayer are all necessary ingredients for life. Struggles come to everyone; it is not a matter of *if*, just a matter of *when*. We are often exposed to Psalm 23, mainly at funeral services, where it is read to assure those who have lost a loved one that there is hope. In my understanding, Psalm 23 is for the living, reassuring the living; yes, even David, a man after God's own heart, walked through the valley of the shadow of death many times, but he knew the Shepherd was there right with him to protect him and lead him to quiet waters.

In our modern societies, there is an increasing trend toward socialized health and welfare, which in a number of European countries is already a way of life (Sweden, Denmark, and, to a degree, in Germany). It had the effect of reliance on the Almighty Government, from the cradle to the grave, so there is less reliance on God. Jesus spoke about the danger of relying on material wealth, neglecting the need to nourish the heart and the soul. Mark 8:36 says, "For what shall it profit a man, if he shall gain the whole world, and lose his own soul?" A full stomach is not the nourishment the soul needs; the soul is strengthened by the instructions and precepts of the Word.

I've taken numerous trips to New York City ministering to the homeless living on the streets of Manhattan and the Bronx, many who at one time have lived in different circumstances. Due to stress stemming from sickness, unemployment, disappointments of some kind, or break-up of the family, they were desperately seeking relief from their situations, turning to alcohol and drugs. Jesus was again calling out, "Come to me, all you who are heavy-laden and burdened, and I will give you rest," or "My peace I give to you; I do not give as the world gives." Jesus gives us peace in the knowledge that we are not alone, he is with us.

How many times have we felt all alone, that no one cares for us, that no one is with us, that we are all alone in this mess, and it manifests itself in loneliness? Mother Teresa of Calcutta wrote: "More people die of loneliness than of hunger." Scripture reminds over and over, "Do not fear, for I am with you," and, "If my God is with me, who can be against me?" The world provides a myriad of cures to heal all our ailments, but the cure for our hearts, soul, and mind is only found in faith and trust in God. Trust in the Lord, and lean not on your own understanding, and he will make your paths straight.

Chapter 7

Struggles

We, the older generation, are many times reminding the younger generation how tough we had it, with many deprivations, but much of what afflicts the younger generation today did not even exist then. There was less temptation from easy access to pornographic material, whether in print or visual media. The pressure to succeed academically and be successful in all that they do comes from their parents. The perfect world expects them to graduate in four years from college and go on to postgraduate school, which burdens many with loans and debts their parents could never have even imagined, and that burden alone leads many to despair and disappointment.

The boomer generation has participated in the greatest money heist in history, the trillions of dollars borrowed by the government to afford them unsustainable benefits and an entitled lifestyle, where the interest payment on the national debt soon exceeds the budget for defense.

The unwillingness of those in power to rein in entitlements, and the lack of political will exhibited by both parties, creates uneasiness and uncertainty about the future for the millennials.

Just imagine for a moment, of the same generation who led and participated in this money scheme, many are churchgoing people and are actively trying to convince the younger generation to follow in their footsteps. That in a strange way would be like me born in Germany during WWII, experiencing the horror their leader has brought upon Germany and the world, and the older generation still encouraging me to embrace the ways of the Third Reich. Strangely enough, I have encountered many a WWII German Veteran who tried to convince me that they could and should have succeeded.

In present-day Germany, the younger generation has turned away from any nationalistic ideology and Christian theology. The conscientious objector deferment rate of draftees during the First Gulf War was close to 80 percent, with the majority opting instead to serve their sixteen-month stint in home care and hospitals. Only three out of my many nephews served in the military.

Especially troubling is the abandonment and unwillingness to practice their faith, foregoing the teaching of the Christian morals and ethics. The statistics of Germans, Catholic, and Protestant alike shows, that 400,000 each year declare before the authorities that they do not believe or attend any religious services, therefore proclaiming that they are atheists and so be released from paying the church tax. In many cases, the main reason is to escape the peculiar church tax, which is 10 percent of their taxable income, and is withheld from their salaries. This tax was instituted by none other than Adolf Hitler under the Concordat of 1933, whereby the Church hierarchy of both denominations was appeased, and no viable opposition emerged to challenge the regime. Dietrich Bonheoffer fought this arrangement and in 1945 was executed for his opposition.

The treaty negotiated between the Vatican and Adolf Hitler was to silence the churches. It was signed on July 21, 1933, by Cardinal Secretary of State Eugenio Pacelli, who later became Pope Pius XII. This Concordat applies to all taxpaying citizens regardless of their faith. There are numerous reasons for the declining number of practicing Christians, but this taxation tops the list for people declaring their atheism and demanding to be exempt from this form taxation.

Jesus was questioned by the Pharisees on whether it was lawful for a Jew to pay taxes to Caesar. Jesus requested a coin and asked whose picture was on it. Looking at the coin, they said "Caesar's." Jesus said: "Give to Caesar what is Caesar's and give to God what belongs to God." Matthew was a tax collector for the Romans, and after meeting Jesus, gave up his post and became a follower of Jesus.

"No one can serve two masters" comes to mind. The present structure in the US of the relationship of church and state, where the state, in return for their power over the church, grants the churches tax exempt status, exercising strong control over the pulpit. Case in point, part of the exempt status prevents the church from speaking out against immoral laws or endorsing any candidates. This unholy alliance has in the past and has especially now produced very serious consequences in public education, colleges, civil courts, and has recently affected free speech, where proselytizing or preaching can be prosecuted for emanating hate, and hate speech was declared unlawful.

Looking in Scripture, you will find the verse where the Word is declared more powerful than a two-edged sword. Hebrews 4:12 says, "For the word of God is quick, and powerful, and sharper than any two-edged sword, piercing even to the dividing asunder of soul and spirit, and of the joints and marrow, and is a discerner of the thoughts and intents of the heart." Is it any wonder why every dictatorship, and now the dictatorship of political correctness, has attacked Scripture as homophobic and intolerant?

One cannot escape the comparison to the Third Reich, where the church stood silently by while their fellow human beings where persecuted and subsequently led to the death chambers. "First they came…" is a poem written by the German Lutheran pastor Martin Niemöller (1892–1984). It is about the cowardice of German intellectuals following the Nazis' rise to power and subsequent incremental purging of their chosen targets, group after group.

> First they came for the socialists, and I did not speak out—
> Because I was not a socialist.
>
> Then they came for the trade unionists, and I did not speak out—
> Because I was not a trade unionist.
>
> Then they came for the Jews, and I did not speak out—
> Because I was not a Jew.

> Then they came for me—and there was no one
> left to speak for me.

I might also add that they came for the mentally challenged, the gypsies, and those who voiced their opposition against the regime. They were called *Volks Verräter*, "a traitor of the people," punishable by death.

Forgive me if I wandered a little back in history, but what I have experienced since the election in 2016 of a new president, where the dialogue, even amongst family and friends, takes an ugly turn once you are outed as a supporter of some of the new president's policies. You are instantly labeled an ignorant, racist, deplorable person; consequently, everyone tiptoes around any subject, and no discussion can and does take place. The self-declared tolerant enlightened have become vehemently intolerant, whether in the media, in social media, in the workplace, or in social circles.

The advice of years gone by was, if you want an enjoyable evening with friends and family, stay away from religion and politics. Religion is these days *Verboten*, "forbidden," and politics is dangerous.

I have been blessed with opportunities in prisons where I am able to deliver a message of love and healing, quoting Scripture like "Love your enemies," and "Enter through the narrow gate. For wide is the gate and broad is the road that leads to destruction, and many enter through it." Or, "The highway to hell is broad; you can enter God's kingdom only through the narrow gate." Many follow the highway to destruction. Recalling the bumper sticker "Drive like hell, you get there sooner" leads me to think of our Interstate Highway System, signs telling us the way to get safely to our destinations.

If we consider the proliferation of the drug culture with its horrific consequences, two young men very close to me and who are in the prime of their life are not able to provide for their own shelter and sustenance, due to either alcohol or drug addiction. When asked, "Why are you doing this to yourself?," the answer is, "Everybody is doing it, so it cannot be bad." So, if more and more of their friends and coworkers are not attending church, in order to fit in, they are also not inclined to explore the meaning of life and eternal life. First

Corinthians 15:32 says, "If the dead are not raised, 'Let us eat and drink, for tomorrow we die'" (NLT). "Whatever works for you. Since there are no absolute truths, I can and will decide what is right for me, without any precepts from Scripture or anyone else."

God's Word does contain absolutes and precepts and commands how we should conduct our lives and have that peace that surpasses all our understanding that only God can provide. Our hearts and minds are not at rest until they rest in God. In wedding vows, couples promise each other: "For better or for worse, in sickness and in health." That has that ring to it, unconditional love no matter what may come. The divorce rate here in the US tells us a different story; many of the divorced are at war with each other and are not amiable.

When we make wedding vows before God, we make a covenant with God, who does not change the law just because the cultural wind changes, or because the laws of the civil authorities are accommodating the preference of the electorate. God's law does not change, and it is very legible. You don't need a Yale graduate lawyer searching for the fine print; that part of God's law is understandable to anyone. Genesis 2:24 says, "Therefore shall a man leave his father and his mother and shall cleave unto his wife: and they shall be one flesh." Mark 10:9 says, "Therefore what God has joined together, let not man put asunder."

Result: children grow up without a mother or father in the home. Where children grow up in single-parent households, especially in poverty-stricken inner cities, high school dropout rates are approaching 50 percent. The result of the breakdown of the family has been well documented, and the evisceration of employment opportunities by way of shutting down factories and reopening them in far-off lands, and the devaluation of religion and faith are the reasons the level of poverty in inner cities has been constant and actually increasing for years.

A strong connection to God the Father, who loves us unconditionally and who never deserts us nor leaves us, and whose office hours are 24/7 for us to call upon, is essential for families to rely upon. It is said that couples who pray together, stay together; this holds true in many cases. When troubles arise, and they will (just think in your own life), if you step back and spend some time in prayer, this time-out permits a more thoughtful response. If we want at all costs proof something, instead of improving the situation, it will in most cases lead to acrimony and resentments, especially with couples who lack the maturity that age and experience provides.

Michele Montaigne wrote: "A perfect marriage is between a wife who is blind and a husband who is deaf." I was told by a comedian: "Marriage is an institution for the blind." I take that as Peter tells us: "Love covers many sins." In other words, we have to be able to overlook and not see every little shortcoming as a reason to break up, as we are all sinners and fall short of the glory of God. That comedian might have had a point.

The love chapter in 1 Corinthians 13:4–8 says, "Love is patient, love is kind. It does not envy, it does not boast, it is not proud. It does not dishonor others, it is not self-seeking, it is not easily angered, it keeps no record of wrongs. Love does not delight in evil but rejoices with the truth. It always protects, always trusts, always hopes, always perseveres. Love never fails." You won't find that anywhere else. Most certainly not in high school or in college or in any other work-related manual.

Ethics today is the name of an academic subject taught only in philosophy departments and professional schools of the university. Until the nineteenth century, colleges offered a course on moral philosophy; it was often the capstone of the curriculum and taught by the college's president.

Education is of utmost importance and it is a lifelong endeavor; so is a relationship with God. Education for the most part teaches us to be productive members of society, contributing to the good of society and all people, whether it is working for someone else or climbing up the corporate ladder and being in charge of many people who rely on their jobs to provide for their families. But how to be a person who is at peace with themselves and their actions and the effect on others may not have been one of the required courses in order to graduate. Ethics and morality are of utmost importance in any leadership position and needed to assure the welfare of those who rely on their jobs to provide for their families and the community thy live in.

CEOs and CFOs are pressed by the stockholders to maximize return on investment, and not only for them but also for themselves through stock options; if the shares go up, they reap huge increases in their portfolio. This has caused ruthless decisions, and countless cities and counties have been severely impoverished, as the factories were shut down and rebuilt in nations where regulations and unions are minimal. This obviously reveals the lack of civic mindedness to their fellow citizens. The decline of the ethical and moral responsibility of the leaders of industry and government has allowed this for many years to continue.

CHAPTER 8

What Is the Reason for Low Church Attendance?

Spiritual priorities have shifted to the occasional ritual, maybe a traditional attendance at Christmas or Easter. The continuous pounding from the media on issues of overpopulation and scarcity of food resources and climate change concerns have been the driving force to forego the starting of families. The 59% absence of millennials from participating in any Christian church life is of great concern, as it has been said that no vacuum ever stays empty, and this is nowhere more evident than in Europe and more so now in the United States. Alternative belief systems are now in the forefront occupying the time allotted for recreation. Islam in particular is filling the vacuum created in Europe by Christian apathy toward the Catholic and Protestant faith communities.

The culture of consumerism and pleasure has taken precedent over the spiritual nourishment of the soul. Due to the low birthrate, abortions, and the lifestyle preferred by the twenty- to fortysomething (because children would severely limit their desire to live a life of pleasure), enter the reality of people living longer, requiring more health care, receiving lengthier Social Security payments, and less and less of the younger generation being there to support those before them.

The European Union has in desperation embarked on an open-border policy, encouraging millions of young men and women to leave their homelands, particularly from Africa and Asia, and make the dangerous journey across deserts and the Mediterranean Sea to reach a very prosperous EU. Most of the immigrants come from devout Islamic nations and are bringing their laws and customs and their way of life with them. Multiple wives, five-time higher birth rates than any European Nation, child marriages, genital mutilations, severe restriction on women's rights—almost without fail, every Islamic nation has a very poor record of human rights.

Western Europe church attendance has seen a decline to the tune of only 3 percent still attending worship services on any given Sunday. Consequently, according to the latest statistics, well over one thousand Christian churches have closed their doors or are converted for secular uses.

In contrast, in the same time frame, 680 new mosques have been erected because there has been such a large influx of young Muslims who take their faith very seriously and do not accept western ways or adhere to democratic laws, especially in regards to women. The Quran explicitly forbids them to integrate their ways and their faith. The Quran contains at least 109 verses that speak of war with nonbelievers, based on their status as non-Muslims. Some are more graphic than others, unfortunately, there are very few verses of tolerance and peace to balance out those calling for nonbelievers to be fought and subdued until they either accept humiliation, convert to Islam, or are killed.

How is it possible that very highly educated young people forfeit their Christian faith and leave a world to their children and grandchildren that disrespects human rights as we know it? The proliferation of the Muslim population has in Europe already risen to a level of power in municipal and state governments, and demand for laws that allow Sharia law practices has come about in a relatively short time, in some countries constituting more than 10 percent, and consequently gaining more influence on the political scene.

Considering some of the passages of the Quran, it is easy to understand their unwillingness to integrate into western society. The Quran (3:56) says, "As to those who reject faith, I will punish them with terrible agony in this world and in the Hereafter, nor will they have anyone to help." Quran (3:151) says, "Soon shall We cast terror into the hearts of the Unbelievers, for that they joined companions with Allah, for which He had sent no authority." Quran (4:76) says, "Those who believe fight in the cause of Allah…" Quran (4:89) says, "They but wish that ye should reject Faith, as they do, and thus be on the same footing (as they): But take not friends from their ranks until they flee in the way of Allah (From what is forbidden). But if they turn renegades, seize them and slay them wherever ye find them; and (in any case) take no friends or helpers from their ranks."

Chapter 9

Islam Versus Christianity

I do not in any way disparage the Muslim faith; all I am pointing out is that it is not compatible with western democracy or Christian faith. Those who are forsaking their Christian faith need to look to the book of Revelation 3:2–3: "Wake up! Strengthen what remains and is about to die, for I have found your deeds unfinished in the sight of my God. Remember, therefore, what you have received and heard; hold it fast, and repent. But if you do not wake up, I will come like a thief, and you will not know at what time I will come to you."

All seven churches mentioned in that chapter of Revelation are no more, and all are located in present-day Turkey, which has been consistently persecuting Christians. Constantinople was the center of Eastern Orthodox Christian faith. The Hagia Sophia, since 1935, nine years after the Republic of Turkey was established by Ataturk, has been operating as a museum by the national government. It reportedly attracts more than three million visitors annually. However, since 2013, some Islamic religious leaders in Turkey have sought to have the Hagia Sophia once again reopened as a mosque.

The question remains: In what kind of world does the millennial generation want to live their old age in, and what kind of world do they want to leave for their sons and daughters and grandchildren??

Christianity has been the bedrock of science, medicine, industrial innovation, arts, laws and democratic institutions which we are benefitting from and enjoy. In the last two thousand years, there have been many periods where the church, people, and nations have faltered and not always followed the teachings of Christ: the

Crusades, the Spanish Inquisition, the Thirty-Year War following the Reformation, the Calvinistic War, and all wars since then. Some wars were to gain freedom from oppression and some for survival.

In many conversations, these discrepancies are brought to the forefront. How much sufferings had occurred in the Christian world. Yes, that is true, but consider that the life afforded at the present time for the average people, especially in Western Europe and the US, is mainly due to Christianity.

If we compare the state of affairs of the average peasant in countries like China and India, Islamic nations and dictatorial nations, explicitly persecuting Christian teaching and assemblies, the need for special glasses is not necessary to see and understand why we would want the Christian faith and its traditions to continue and allow us to live in a land that has a Bill of Rights guaranteeing life, liberty, and the pursuit of happiness.

Erwin Lutzer, pastor of Moody Church in Chicago wrote *When a Nation Forgets God*, taking Germany as an example through the years, from the 1920s to the rise of the Nazi Regime, leading to the destruction of Germany in 1945. What happens when God is supplanted with leaders who are enacting laws that are contrary to the laws of God? The US is well on the way of repeating what was wrong then and is still wrong now. The Nuremberg Laws (Nürnberger Gesetze) were anti-Semitic and racial laws in Nazi Germany. They were enacted by the Reichstag on September 15, 1935, and extended in 1938 to legalize the extermination of millions.

The German Supreme Court ruled that Jewish people are not human and made it legal to eradicate them; it was the beginning of the Holocaust: no life, no liberty, and no pursuit of happiness for different people, only the chosen ones, i.e., the Aryan race, the "Master Race." This led to the murdering of Jewish people and all opposition; mentally challenged Germans and Slavic people were degraded as *Untermenschen*, a subhuman class of people.

Here in the US, a similar law was enacted and blessed by the Supreme Court that permits abortion on demand. The US Supreme Court in 1973 found it necessary to declare a fetus *not* a human being; if it would declare a fetus as a human being, then it would be unconstitutional according to the Bill of Rights, which says we are endowed by our Creator with an inalienable right to life, liberty, and the pursuit of happiness. Opinion of the court written by Supreme Court Justice Blackmun, "We need not resolve the difficult question of when life begins. When those trained in the respective disciplines of medicine, philosophy, and theology are unable to arrive at any consensus, the judiciary, at this point in the development of man's knowledge, is not in a position to speculate as to the answer." Since that time, 60 million babies have been aborted. Abortion up to the moment of birth is now legal in New York State and celebrated by the media as progress. No-fault divorce is established, and recently the politicians are counting on the millennial votes to expand their powers and enable them to enact laws that are contrary to Christian worldview and biblical teachings. When civil laws are substituted for biblical laws, it opens the door for all kinds of dictatorships, restricting freedom of speech and freedom of religion.

Chapter 10

Redistribution of Resources

The American mainline churches are across the board in decline. Many of the contributors are aged, and many have passed away. The funds of those who passed away and given to the church are tied up in endowments and are restricted to the maintenance of the church structures and specific purposes, which prohibits the use of the funds for the evangelization of the young, who are exposed to the gospel according to TV. The media is indoctrinating young people and reaching them in record numbers on the Internet 24/7 with the relentless ads and shows and speakers who are advocating alternative lifestyles, and a message of no absolutes: if it feels good, you can do it. The amount of money spent on this type of indoctrination seems to have no limits.

The point I am trying to make is this: whatsoever the media culture can muster, in no way can it match the power of God and the overwhelming resources available by Christian churches to spread the gospel according to God. Just think of David and Goliath: the Israelites saw a big enemy, but what David saw was a small enemy standing against his big God. David said, "Who is this uncircumcised Philistine that he should defy the armies of the living God?"

Christians outnumber those who want to outlaw Christian values and persecute Christians in the public square, calling them homophobic, bigoted, racists. Christians are hiding in their churches, sincerely believing in God and in the teachings of Jesus Christ, but are now irrelevant in the modern culture. The sacrament of marriage instituted by God is too restrictive and severely infringing on their cohabitation and sexual practices and preferences.

A massive effort will be necessary to counter this dismantling of Christian values and the Christian faith. Consider the Book of Acts: if a small band of believers was able to change the then-known world ruled by evil rulers and being persecuted mercilessly, and those Christians did prevail, why does it seem to be insurmountable today? Not too long ago, we saw the demise of the Soviet Empire falling under its own evil practices. The gift and power of the media and the digital capabilities are gifts from God and available today to Christians as it is for those who are on a warpath against Christianity.

The bunker mentality, seeking safety, sitting in church on Sunday, listening to fiery speeches and charismatic entertainment, and then the rest of the week internalizing but not externalizing their faith is reminiscent of the Communist regimes restricting Christians to worship within the four walls of their home, but not in the public square. We are now here in the US acting freely in like manner all by ourselves and are acquiescing quietly to the politically correct enforcement police.

Public prayers are frowned upon, crosses are removed from public squares and are viewed with dismay as it may intimidate a nonbeliever, the name of Jesus cannot be spoken in any public speech, and prayers in public schools are strictly forbidden.

In my walk with the Lord, it became obvious to me that to counter this change in public worship, I needed to find a venue to bring the good news to as many people as I can with the time available to me. That opportunity to bring the good news and the benefits of living a life pleasing to God could not happen in the traditional form of being a valuable member of my local church. My desire to share something that good was overwhelming for me and not much opportunity was provided in ways of outreach.

The churches' main purpose should be the mentoring and equipping of the faithful to bring glory to God. I am thoroughly convinced that is the reason the Lord told the disciples: "I will tear down this temple and rebuild it in three days." If the destruction of the temple had not occurred, the Diaspora would not have occurred either. The Jewish people were dispersed all over the earth; they traveled on roads the Romans built, and the disciples followed in their tracks. We read in Acts that wherever they went, they went to the synagogues and proclaimed the Way. And in the same way, something drastic will have to happen to move those who so convincingly proclaim their faith in church on Sunday to go out and convince people young and old of the way of Jesus Christ.

Matthew chapter 7 is a stark reminder of what happens to people who are enthusiastically singing and dancing, only to find out what Jesus would say to them before him: "I never knew you. Away from me, you evildoers."

I have for the last twenty-five years shared the gospel in maximum-security prisons, youth prisons, mental hospitals, city hospitals, and old-age homes and hospices; I in no way want to be recognized for this, but I desire to tell anyone willing to listen, I thank the Lord every day for the privilege of being alive and able to share this incomparable love with the least of these.

Twenty-four years ago, I was taking part of a homeless outreach ministry on the streets of New York City. At around 1:30 a.m., I was searching for homeless people under the East River Highway, and walking down between the pylons with blankets and sandwiches and some toiletries, a very large and mean-looking dog charged at me. In desperation, I called out, "I am here from the church with food and blankets. If you call the dog back, I will bring it to you." The man sitting in the dark between the cement pylons called the dog back, and as I approached the man, I saw the biggest toothless smile and the warmest person. As I sat down next to the man and looked at him, I saw the face of Jesus in that man's face.

That night, I could not find sleep. I prayed with a bunkmate almost through the whole night. That night I realized that the only way we can change the world and experience God is by going out and reaching out, especially to those who have been marginalized, and those who have been brainwashed and indoctrinated by the postmodern culture.

I sincerely believe the harvest is plentiful, but the workers are way too few. Sitting in church on Sundays and dressing in their finest and maybe even having a sumptuous coffee hour afterward in the fellowship hall is, to say the least, not as challenging as going out to where the lost are. I am tempted to use a secular approach in evangelizing, that of a vacuum cleaner salesman. Christianity is the best product on the market, but unless we convince the young millennials of the overwhelming benefit derived from living with a biblical worldview, and if it is replaced with a secular worldview, they may not wake up until it is too late. The love of Christ far surpasses anything the world has to offer, especially to the people who are desperately in need of a peace that surpasses human understanding.

Jesus told everyone who would listen, "I am the way, the truth, and the life. Come to me, all who are heavy-laden and burdened, and I will give you rest." Without his rest and the peace that comes from the Lord Jesus, many will reach for drugs or anything that will provide them with a temporary fix or peace and a little relaxation. Many are looking for love and peace in all the wrong places, as a country song many years ago crooned.

Chapter 11

What Kind of World Would the Millennial Generation Want to Leave for Their Children and Grandchildren?

What kind of a world do we want to live in, and what kind of world do we want to leave to our children and grandchildren? A secular society and culture without a biblical moral compass and precepts will, without any doubt, find itself in a downward spiral. In all of man's history, vacuums have never stayed empty; they were always filled. Question is, what and who will fill the empty space? Ever since the garden of Eden, there never had been another perfect world, and no man has ever been able to provide one, no matter what the promises claimed. History is full of junkyards of manmade empires; all claimed that it will be heaven on earth, or Nirvana, or Shangri La. Man cannot provide what only God can provide. The question is, with all the modern tools available, the mobility possible with airplanes and fiber-optic communication enabling us to send a message around the globe in seconds, why is the faith community not using these advanced technologies more effectively?

Could it be that the evil forces have a monopoly on the talented individuals, enticing them with salaries and comfort the average person can only dream about?

What is at stake here is more valuable than anything Silicon Valley can promise, the forgiveness of sins and the hope of everlasting life in the presence of the Lord. Everyone has a divine appointment before God, no exception granted, no billions are accepted as a bribe for entry into the heavenly kingdom. I have seen, in my many years of serving as a hospital pastoral care volunteer, how many young lives are cut short in the prime of their lives. But I see my mission more for what kind of life is available while still here on earth! The inmates in the prisons I visit are spending a good portion of their lives behind bars, some even resemble cages, but they are children of God, and God wants them to have hope and a future. He wants to prosper them, not harm them (Jer. 29:11).

And many people who are not incarcerated are so beholden of their lifestyle that they are prisoners to their way of life, and believing that they are living life to the fullest, being misled by the herd mentality, everybody is grasping for more stuff to possess or own.

A bumper sticker I recently saw: "He who has the most toys wins." Or the adage: "Hard work got me where I am, but where the hell am I?" Jesus tells us: "Wide is the road to destruction, but narrow is the way." Go in through the narrow gate that leads to life; wide is the road that leads to destruction, and many people are entering by it (Matthew 7:13).

Leo Tolstoy, the author of *War and Peace*, is a good example. With all his success and influence in the Russian elite at the time, he was a very unhappy man. In the 1870s, Tolstoy experienced a profound moral crisis. He had attained fame and wealth, and yet he was contemplating suicide. Later, as he was observing the simple faith of the peasants and the happiness they possessed, he realized it was their simple faith that was the reason for their joy.

There needs to be a balance in every life. Someone can be a very zealous worshipper. That is where the expression comes from: "He is so heavenly that he is no earthly good," or someone is overly possessed by their desire to gain the whole world, but in the process loses his soul.

The time we spend in prayer or in church is if we want to call a time-out, a time to contemplate, take a break. Remember McDonald's slogan of years ago, "You deserve a break today." You don't just deserve it, you need it. It gives time to examine our priorities: are we spending enough quality time with those we love, or are we using every single ounce of our energy in amassing wealth that can be gone in a flash or a sudden downturn on Wall Street? Do we make time to enjoy social events or charitable works?

We find a life worth living when we follow Jesus's command: "Let your light so shine before men, that they may see your good works, and glorify your Father which is in heaven" (Matthew 5:16). This is the secret to a life worth living.

Chapter 12

The Modern Family

How is it humanly possible to wear multiple hats and not look funny or out of kilter? But it is not funny at all when young families with little children are forced to wear many hats. Consider a young mother: she is in many cases required to work a full-time job, manage a household, be a whatever mom (soccer, football, basketball, piano lessons, taxi driver, etc.), driving children to daycare, picking the children up, battling traffic congestions, and being the food purveyor, cook, and housekeeper, and, as humanly possible, able muster enough energy for little liaison with her spouse.

The husband in many families, being supportive, shares many of the necessary chores before he leaves for his full-time job. In today's environment, a good paying job requires total commitment to their career, and in many cases, travels away from home, which leaves additional burdens on the spouse left at home.

I look back to the time before the seventies, when one paycheck was enough to allow a mom to be home for the children when they came from school, maybe a part-time job some evenings after the husband came home from work to augment or save for a family trip. This was the world my wife and I lived in when our children were small. I worked overtime on Saturday mornings so that my wife could stay home with the children and not have to go to work outside the home. We mutually agreed that her presence in the home was of utmost importance for the children; they knew that when they walked through the door after school and called out, "*Mom*," she was there.

The shuffling of children from one place to another every single day does have an impact on their lives. A hired help is in charge of their children's development throughout most of their waking hours, and parents tend to let their children up longer so that they can spend more time with them, which in turn lessens the time that the couple can attend to each other's needs.

The supervision of a parent over their children's activities is in this digital age even more critical, as they can and will be exposed to material which, not too long ago, parents would never have exposed their children to and never would have dreamed could be beamed into our homes. People would never have invited this kind of language and pictures into their homes. The language that is permissible on TV or the porno industry that is so easily available on the computer has invaded the language used even by kindergarteners to the point that Sunday school teachers are hard to find because of the use of very foul language heard in class from small children.

Foul and dirty language is now protected by the free mandates; restrictions are nonexistent or have been removed or not enforced. There was actually family time, when questionable materials were relegated to a later hour.

The millennial generation I am addressing here has an almost mission impossible to regain some civility and tranquility in the society they live in. In my chaplain volunteer work in a youth mental hospital and youth prison, I see the fallout and the consequences children are suffering from the changing lifestyles. I am not referring to the gay rights movement, but cohabitation without commitment, and multiple partners in the lives of their mother or fathers. How can a child experience normalcy, trying to adjust to complete strangers living in their homes? In many cases they are being abused and molested by their parent's partners, not being protected by their mother, who hates to lose her new boyfriend for a myriad of reasons—inflamed passion, economic necessity—and allows it to happen.

In years past, it was more the Cinderella story: dad remarried, and Cinderella was neglected. But that was in storybooks. In the present culture, this is now the norm as an enormous number of couples are creating what is now called a blended family with not only one more sibling but possibly three or more. It might seem reasonable in a TV show, but not in the real world, where each child feels the effects of limited resources and tribal competition for attention and later for tuitions. The number of children who grow up in single-parent household families increases every year: 14 percent in 1960, 19 percent in 1980, 34 percent in 2010, 43 percent in 2018. That means boys and girls do not have the guidance and attention of their mother or father in their formative and arguably the most difficult time in their lives.

This might be the result of what came to be known the Murphy Brown Syndrome, where a husband is not necessary to raise a child; on TV, a part-time house painter was quite enough. Not in any episode was the issue of faith or church attendance even remotely mentioned. God and church have been systematically eliminated out of the TV shows and movies, and alternative lifestyles are portrayed as the new norm. Maybe it is the new norm; question remains, since these lifestyles do not provide the necessary procreation numbers to sustain a social construct for a secure social security system, how will that issue be addressed? It is said that "figures never lie, but many liars figure," which means we are continuously misinformed about the consequences of lifestyles that are against natural law.

Adding the number of aborted babies into the equation, it becomes obvious that this fairytale is not sustainable. In recent years, the same members of society ascribing to this new lifestyle are vehemently advocating unlimited immigration, legal or illegal, to raise the numbers of voters to afford them the continuance of their ideology of no absolutes.

I was born in Germany near the end of WWII, started first grade in 1948, graduating in 1957 from elementary school, and entered vocational school in April of 1957, and graduated in 1960. I married my wife Roswitha in 1963 in Germany, and on August 22, boarded a ship and immigrated to the US.

The importance of faith in the lives of people who were living in the aftermath of WWII is manifested in how they managed to survive under the worst circumstances one could experience, and still were able to rebuild their lives and their country.

The masses clung to their faith, Protestants and Catholics alike; it was pure and simple faith in their God that sustained them, and he did. The German *Wirtschafts-Wunder* was so named because it was an "Economic Miracle," rising out of the ashes left by American and British bombers after destroying most of the cities and factories.

America also recovered from the hardships of WWII, especially the shortages and deprivations of food, cars, and consumer goods; and the people also rebuilt their lives and their nation into the most powerful nation on earth.

The majority of children grew up in homes where the work ethic was impressed upon their children. Many parents where survivors of the Great Depression era, arguably the worst of time for the people of America. That experience taught the parents the value of hard work and this was passed on to their children and embraced. Faith played an important role in the fabric of the American family life; there were things children would not engage in as it would have chagrined their parents. People attended Bible teaching and believed that there would be a day of reckoning for our actions.

David the Psalmist in Psalm 51 came before God and declared, "For I know my transgressions, and my sin is always before me and done what is evil in your sight." Try as we might, laws enacted by a government are there to be circumvented; that is human nature. Adam and Eve are a prime example. God laid down the law, yet they were easily misled by the evil one into to doubting God's instruction.

In the world today, governments have laid down millions of laws, and humans are still enticed by the evil one to ignore them. A very good example is the speed limit posted on the Interstate Highways. If it is posted as 65 miles per hour, safe to say that it is uniformly ignored; the only explanation possible is that there is either a severe vision problem, illiterate drivers, or no motivation to obey the law that was enacted for their own safety.

Even God recognized the fact that a written law is ineffective. Jeremiah 33 says, "This is the new covenant I will make with the house of Israel after that time, declares the Lord. I will put my law in their minds and write it on their hearts." The laws the authorities are trying to enforce are only effective when the people are obeying them with their hearts and minds.

Since 1973, the Supreme Court of the US has legalized laws that are contrary to the laws of God; in other words, usurping the authority of God. As one Connecticut congresswoman explained on TV, we should not blame the courts and the government for enacting laws that the lifestyles of people demand. In this manner, the law of the Lord was declared irrelevant to the modern society as it does not conform to ways that people want to live their lives. Can you imagine the implications this has on the younger generation seeing their parents, brothers, and sisters living in situations unimaginable fifty years ago?

In recent years, people were even being chastised for trying to live by biblical principles and are denied the opportunity of being appointed or elected to a governing position. What was an admirable way of life has now become a detriment. What was good has now been declared evil, and what was evil has now been declared good. The media and the press are on a 24/7 mission to reeducate and completely displace biblical teaching from the public square, the ACLU litigating any public display of the Ten Commandments from courthouses and public buildings and parks.

Question arises: who is benefitting from a life where God's laws are discarded and are no absolutes?

Law enforcement cannot and will not be able to enforce all laws; there simply will never be enough funds and police forces if the public does not respect the laws and rules and regulations. When the autonomy of God is ignored, anarchy is the likely result, or worse, as in post-WWI in Europe and Russia, dictatorships emerged promising reestablishment of new law and new order. This is not ancient history, but only a hundred years ago.

Chapter 13

The Critical Importance of Christianity to Western Culture?

Buddhism in China; Hinduism in India; Islam in much of Asia, North Africa, and the Middle East; seventy years of Communism in the Soviet Union, and twelve years of the promised Third Reich in Germany are ample evidence of the lack of human rights when Christian principals and Christianity is suppressed or outright persecuted: China's disastrous result of the one-child family policy, India's Hindu caste system, and Islamic suppression of woman's rights to education and equal rights under the Sharia Law.

Chapter 14

Question: Why Would a Highly Developed Western University Demonize Christianity?

Universities Have Their Origin in Christianity!

Could it be that Christianity cannot be conformed to the alternative lifestyles promoted and propagated by the intellectual elite? Conservative lectors and speakers are routinely forbidden or denied the same open forums eagerly made available to left-leaning speakers. Open discussions are shouted down or disrupted to the point that colleges and universities are using safety concerns and security as the reason for not accommodating conservative speakers.

Free speech is therefore subverted under the guise of safety concerns and students are denied the experience of listening to viewpoints not of their own in a civilized manner, which is critical to their being able to develop a more balanced understanding of the world they live in. If "shouting down" or public disorder becomes the norm in preventing opposing viewpoints of a platform for open dialogue, what travesty that would be for the cherished first amendment of free speech?

To use a German song from Hoffman von Fallersleben:

> Die Gedanken sind frei, wer kann sie erraten,
> sie fliehen vorbei wie nächtliche Schatten.
> Kein Mensch kann sie wissen, kein Jäger
> erschießen, es bleibet dabei: die Gedanken sind frei.

Translated in summary: "All worldly powers cannot kill free thinking; you can kill the thinker but not the thoughts."

The opportunity to share their thoughts publicly has allowed the thinkers of this world to impact the world around them. Dictators have routinely suppressed any open discussion that would deviate from their own ideology. Alexander Solzhenitsyn wrote *The Gulag Archipelago: An Experiment in Literary Investigation*, for which he was awarded the Nobel Prize for Literature. Germany lost many of their greatest physicists during the Nazi regime. Books of Jewish authors were burned in public squares, synagogues were burned and critics of their actions were sent to concentration camps for reeducation, or, as in many cases, killed. China has never fully recuperated from the disaster of the "Cultural Revolution," which decimated the educated class in a horrific display of demeaning rites of intellectuals, beating them and publicly shaming them, marching teachers and professors through the streets of the cities and then banning them to labor camps.

Chapter 15

One Might Ask

How could a five-thousand-year-old culture stoop so low? We might be smug and say, "This would never happen here in the US." Well, think again. How many people in very high positions have fallen under the accusations and innuendos, even those that could not be substantiated, and are publicly convicted, demoted, and removed from their positions? We see the repercussions already happening. Very capable people would not expose themselves to such a kangaroo court of public scrutiny by the political enemies of whomsoever nominated them and then have to withdraw with their reputation in shambles.

No one person alive is up and above this kind of character assassination. Romans 3:23 says, "We are sinners, for all have sinned and fall short of the glory of God." Even in many cases, where people have apologized for something that they did or were part of twenty to forty years ago, the lynch mob demands blood as the bare minimum; mercy is not in their vocabulary. Politically correct expressions are absolutely necessary and opposing viewpoints have to be silenced.

I have personally experienced this in my own family. It is much safer to discuss trivial subjects like the weather, a movie, or food, only if it does not impact the environment in any way. The joy of eating can be lost when someone considers the damage done to the environment and the impact raising cattle has on climate change. The pinnacle of this kind of irrationality is that some states are considering the taxation of livestock and ending the raising of cattle altogether. Vegetarians, vegans, and animal lovers are on the lookout for those who still enjoy traditional meals. Well, someone wrote, if the vegans love animals so much, then why are they eating their food?

Consider the passage in the Book of Acts 10:10–14: "Peter became hungry and wanted something to eat, and while the meal was being prepared, he fell into a trance. He saw heaven opened and something like a large sheet being let down to earth by its four corners. It contained all kinds of four-footed animals, as well as reptiles and birds. Then a voice told him, 'Get up, Peter. Kill and eat.' 'Surely not, Lord!' Peter replied. 'I have never eaten anything impure or unclean.' The voice spoke to him a second time, 'Do not call anything impure that God has made clean.'"

The Bible tells us to kill and eat. Would the desire to follow biblical principles be responsible for the global warming and cause the ice caps to melt and the seas to rise? I wonder if anyone has even studied the impact of stopping animal husbandry, shutting down beef and dairy farms in all the lands, and outlawing and ending hunting seasons. I am making a little light of this, as this could be disastrous for the industrial as well as for the developing world. Maybe, just maybe, the elite followers of this theory are not living in the real world or are in a trance as the apostle Peter was and not aware of the ramifications this would cause or entail.

There are at this writing approximately 7.6 billion people on this earth and soon maybe 8 or 9 billion people. How would they be nourished, considering all the different customs and eating habits? We would inevitably arrive and already are nearing the final solution to the overcrowding of the earth by promoting abortions and euthanasia. That still brings up the issue of travel and transportation to and from work, earning a living, and financial stability.

The term *final solution* has a terrible reputation. The Third Reich attempted to find the final solution and has murdered millions of people that were deemed expendable and undesired. The Wannsee Conference was a meeting of senior government officials of Nazi Germany leaders, held in the Berlin suburb of Wannsee on January 20, 1942. The purpose of the conference was the implementation of the final solution to the Jewish question, whereby most of the Jews of German-occupied Europe would be deported to occupied Poland and murdered in extermination camps.

This scenario was not experienced in some faraway tribal land in Papua New Guinea, or in the Amazon jungle. No, it was in a modern European nation that planned to repopulate the world with the Superior Master Race, without undesirables to use valuable resources. This idea was actually attempted in the US under the eugenics experiment and enthusiastically copied by Germany, arguably one of the most advanced societies at the time. Many African Americans were, without their consent, sterilized with the intended purpose in the final analysis to reduce the inferior African Americans from overpopulating. Compulsory sterilization laws where adopted by over thirty states, which led to more than 60,000 sterilizations.

The abandoning of biblical teaching allows a new breed of intellectuals to devise and introduce a new world order where nothing is impossible, and no absolutes stand in the way or hinder the advancement of this new world order. If God is minimized and relegated to the privacy of the home and effectively banned from the public square, nothing will stand in the way. The religious community is in many ways already cowering under the weight of public condemnation for their bigoted and homophobic teachings of biblical standards and are condemned as irrelevant in the scheme of this modern society. Romans chapter 1 and Leviticus chapter 18 place restrictions on what is permissible in sexual relationships.

I sincerely wish that I would have an answer to how far away from biblical principles this postmodernism culture will move and the consequences it will bring with it. The only clue that I can gather is gleaming in the Old Testament, as the chosen people have disobeyed God and built pagan altars, sacrificing their children on those altars, and many times being subjected to other pagan nations once conquered and then forced to adopt pagan practices; only then in their desperation did they call on Yahweh to remember them and set them free.

Psalm 137:1–9 reads, "By the rivers of Babylon we sat and wept when we remembered Zion. There on the poplars we hung our harps, for there our captors asked us for songs, our tormentors demanded songs of joy; they said, 'Sing us one of the songs of Zion!' How can we sing the songs of the Lord while in a foreign land? If I forget you, Jerusalem, may my right hand forget its skill. May my tongue cling to the roof of my mouth if I do not remember you, if I do not consider Jerusalem my highest joy." The prophets Isaiah and Jeremiah repeatedly warned the Israelites of the impending disaster, but they would not heed their calls.

Since the old wisdom that history will repeat itself over and over is so true, people forget the ordinances and commandments of God, and then, after suffering under horrible conditions, like in Psalm 137:1–9, lamenting in Babylonian captivity and calling out to God, by the intervention of God are able to rebuild their shattered lives and nation.

My hope and prayers are that this scenario would not befall western society and that the Bible precepts have not been completely removed and vanished, so nations will be able to reestablish the principals and admonitions of the Lord. (A good read is Thomas Cahill's *How the Irish Saved Civilization: The Untold Story of Ireland's Heroic Role from the Fall of Rome to the Reintroduction of Christianity into Medieval Europe*.)

The precepts of the Lord never fail us in our private lives nor in the nations that proclaim "One Nation Under God," or the swearing-in at the inaugurations, "So help me, God." Both of those customs are under severe attack. The generation who grew up and lived under the teaching of the commandments of the Bible are now in the minority or are dying off in record numbers due to old age, which leaves the millennial generation in a position of power and influence.

This cannot be overstated enough; they are the finished product of these changes that have been taught to them from grade school on all the way up to their time in college. And it does not end there; the already infused culture is pervasive in the family, workplace, social functions, the media, and cyberspace. If you are a Facebook user, you are inundated with New Age worshippers. Traditional views of a time gone by are not welcome. I am not referring to the ancients; no, just one generation ago.

Ronald Reagan warned us what happens to our freedom: "Freedom is never more than one generation away from extinction. It doesn't pass on to our children in the bloodstream, it must be fought for, protected, and handed down to them to do the same, or one day the older generation will spend their sunset years telling their children and children's children what it was once like to live in the United States, where people were free of politically tyranny and lament like the Israelites in captivity. We sit by the rivers of a once great America and weep when we remember that it once was the land of the free and the home of the brave."

Christianity is disappearing fast in the public square. It took only one generation to take prayer out of our schools and public functions; high school and college graduations cannot include any reference to Jesus or faith in him. Our freedom to worship is now restricted to home or to the inside of a church building, and voicing biblical texts concerning unnatural laws is chastised as homophobic. Politically incorrect expressions are labeled "hate speech" and is punishable by law.

Who decides what is considered hate speech? Is it the political party in power or the prevailing sympathy and the desires of the elite establishment? Obviously, the Deplorables, so labeled by Hillary Clinton, are not in lockstep with the enlightened liberal elite. The freedom of expression of thought and ideas is strictly *verboten*. College auditoriums are denied to anyone not promoting the new ideology or postmodernism.

The Definition of Postmodernism

Postmodernism is a philosophy that says absolute truth does not exist. Supporters of postmodernism deny long-held beliefs and conventions and maintain that all viewpoints are equally valid. Today, postmodernism has led to relativism, the idea that all truth is relative. There is no such thing as absolute truth, but the truth is that if someone runs into the path of a train and dies as a result of their action, he or she will be dead; it is the simplest example that absolute truth does exist, and that you will die if you ignore absolute truth.

Jesus's statement, "I am the truth, the way, and life," can be debated or questioned, but it does not change the truth; only our interpretation of what truth is can be reinterpreted and changed. Now we are faced with all these aberrations of different lifestyles, and unfortunately the health risks and the burden upon the society to provide long-term care if necessary, as in the case of motorcyclists who refuse to wear helmets. Brain injuries are 90 percent irreversible and require long-term care the rest of their lives and a massive amount of funds that the injured party in almost all instances is never able to shoulder.

The postmodern mantra that love makes a family poses the question, where does it start and where does it end? The free love of the hippy generation has provided us an inkling of the possibilities: no commitment, anywhere and everywhere, induced by LSD or cannabis or heroin. Children are living in very unstable circumstances; it may consist of a converted VW bus or a communal arrangement where the children are unsure who their natural mother or father is.

Quoting from John Stonestreet of Colson Center for Christian Worldview: "Many of us predicted polyamory would, in fact, be the next cause of the sexual revolution. Polyamorous marriage seems, for now, inevitable. That would mean marriage between more than two people, and why not? If marriage is officially severed from procreation, as so-called 'same-sex marriage' has now been legislated, then there is no reason to keep it to two people, three, four, or more."

There are no boundaries to any combination; someone may proclaim, "I love my sister" or "I love my daughter" or "We are enjoying a multiple arrangement of open sexual relations with all the inhabitants in any living arrangement." I know that I may be carrying this too far, but think for a moment what we have seen in recent times; what was considered impossible just one generation ago is now the law of the land and considered normal. Question is: What is the new normal going to be and what will it look like in another generation?

JOSEF HERZ

Enter the Islamization of the Western Christian Civilization!

One does not have to have any anti-Islamic agenda to raise serious doubt about the influx of Muslims into Western Europe or the US to learn what the consequences will be. One only has to take Pakistan, Saudi Arabia, and Iran into consideration: overwhelmingly Islamic, not one of them has any resemblance to democracy, and all have a dismal human rights records. Islamic faith in all these countries is state-mandated, and any opposition is a violation punishable by death.

Women's rights are severely restricted, seen alone by the fact that when a woman brings accusations against a man, she needs two witnesses as opposed to one witness required for a male who accuses a woman. Compared to any western Christian society, a human right is whatever Mohammed decreed. He was a man who found it permissible by God to marry a child, and authorized in the Holy Book the slaughter of anyone unwilling to convert or who disagreed with Mohammed's teaching.

Free speech is nonexistent, and as in the case of Afghanistan, the education of girls was not allowed until the overthrow of the Taliban, and is now in danger of being repealed. So, my humble question is this: what system would the new postmodern society like to live under, instead of Christianity?

If we look at the advancement of medicine; industrial advancement of engineering consumer goods; availability of jobs manufacturing autos, machinery, and new inventions, to name just a few; computers and communications equipment—as far as to my knowledge, none of these mentioned originated in an Islamic country. Western Christian countries have led the west for centuries; the third world has not prospered as has the west. Colonialism has most certainly played a part for the underdevelopment of India. The caste system has kept the majority of their people in difficult straits, unable to rise above their circumstances. This is contrary to Hollywood elites, who believe in a Nirvana of some kind.

The same cannot be said about China, where emperors and warlords have ruled until Communism replaced them, and has been even more oppressive. Islamic countries have regressed from their heights in the eighth century. The Islamic Golden Age was a period of cultural, economic, and scientific flourishing in the history of Islam, traditionally dated from the eighth century to the fourteenth century. This period is traditionally understood to have begun during the reign of the Abbasid Caliph Harun al-Rashid (AD 786–809) with the inauguration of the House of Wisdom in Baghdad, where scholars from various parts of the world with different cultural backgrounds were mandated to gather and translate all of the world's classical knowledge into the Arabic language. This period ended with the collapse of the Abbasid Caliphate due to Mongol invasions and the Siege of Baghdad in AD 1258. A few contemporary scholars place the end of the Islamic Golden Age as late as the end of fifteenth to sixteenth centuries.

The masses of China and India have prospered with the introduction of open markets and the infusion of western technologies and inventions, but there is no comparison between the US or Western Europe standard of living that the masses enjoy, as a matter of fact. This is not meant to belittle the Asian cultures, they have a lot to teach us in many different areas, but when we consider the average people's condition and living standard, then the obvious conclusion and question should be *why*? Why the stark difference?

Why would the millennial generation even consider replacing Christianity, without being sure what the end result will look like, whatever it may be? Will it be a "trail-mix offering," where you can pick and choose some bits and pieces but ignore the rest?

Christianity has provided the foundational structure for families to raise their children; abandon that structure and society will literally be in a free fall and open to any and all interpretations of what makes a family. Hillary Clinton coined the slogan, "It takes a village to make a family." This has a ring of some kind of communal arrangement. The traditional family is a father and mother married to each other in a covenantal commitment and living under one roof, providing a stable environment for children to grow up in and develop into productive adults. Obviously, nothing is ever perfect and never will be, but when broken and uncertain conditions become the norm, or the new normal, consequences can be much worse, much less be foreseen, and may be impossible to correct later.

Question: Why travel the road to uncertainty, or better yet, the road not taken?

Chapter 16

The Polarization of America

Illegal Immigration

We are at this moment in time faced with a liberal establishment that is advocating open borders and illegal immigration without concerns for the legal inhabitants, their health, their welfare, and their wealth and safety. A nation without secure borders is not a nation; ignoring sound immigration laws will ultimately lead to a breakdown of society, making it impossible to arrest and prosecute criminals and safeguard legal citizens' lives.

The US has entered a whole new phase of immigration issues arising out of the chaotic circumstances in South American countries like Guatemala, Honduras, and Nicaragua from where hundreds of thousands of people are fleeing through Mexico and entering the US illegally in large numbers, which presents a significant security and safety issue for the American public. Many are just poor people fleeing the drug-filled and corrupt political culture that has spread in those countries; they are seeking a safe haven for their families. The US still is and always has been welcoming immigrants from all over the world, providing they intend to enter the country legally and through the proper channels.

The proper enforcement of immigration law has been undermined by a corrupt American political system that encourages illegal entries in to the US for the sole purpose of swelling the voter registration numbers without the proper documents. States have not enforced voter identification requirements and therefore encouraged foreigners to vote for whomsoever provides the most benefits that are not meant for people in the country illegally but for the native-born.

The same people who advocate open borders and unlimited immigration are the same people who live in mansions surrounded and secured by ten-foot walls and fences but expose the average citizens to the dangers of immigrants who may have criminal records or untreated diseases that have been eradicated in the US many years ago. This has increased much animosity toward people from Latin America and foreigners in general.

People are leaving their native lands because of the drug-induced violence and the corrupt governments. The question arises, why is the corruption so endemic in these countries? Well, you could argue, there is a general culture of ignoring their laws, and gang activity has infiltrated all levels of society and governing bodies in these countries. The immigrants leaving their homeland and entering the US illegally are ignoring US laws, not complying with US immigration authorities, and not reporting to hearings in immigration courts to determine their legality. According to the courts' reporting, 90 percent are disappearing in the general population and working illegally without paying taxes or health insurance but are demanding free schooling for their children and free health care that is not readily available to the hardworking American taxpayers.

You could argue that the very lawless and corrupt circumstances they left behind are now brought and transplanted to their host country. Criminal gangs engaged in drug smuggling and general criminal activity are so prevalent that, at the time of this writing, illegal criminals are the largest group inhabiting American prisons.

Millions upon millions of immigrants entered the US in the last two hundred years, awaiting their turn. Immigration laws state that any criminal activity or public assistance would be cause for eviction back to their homeland. Approximately ten million are living illegally in the US and are not accounted for. The last four Republican and Democrat administrations have allowed this situation and even encouraged the practice by spreading the word that all you have to do is make it somehow across the border, disappear, and find work on the black market.

National enterprises from agricultural to food-processing companies to construction, small and large, are benefitting from employing illegals and fail at E-Verifying. Large sums of political contributions are responsible for pressuring their elected officials not to enforce existing laws, thus enabling industries to employ large numbers without proper registry, no social security, and no health insurance. They are then the sole responsibility of the unsuspecting public for their health and welfare.

This situation is already impacting elections, especially in California, New Mexico, Texas, and New York. With the unlawful practice of declaring states and cities "sanctuaries," hindering ICE from evicting dangerous criminals who harm American citizens and visitors overstaying their visas, have all created a very dangerous situation that this new administration is now trying to correct. Congress is fighting the president tooth and nail, engaging district courts in overturning executive orders and preventing the immigrants from gaining legal status, and by that, enabling employers to continue to profit and retain power over these poor immigrants.

My biggest fear is that a leader will be elected who promises a change. Adolf Hitler was swept into power by the chaos that people endured following WWI, and if my memory serves me correctly, every dictatorial regime has their origins in the same scenario; the Weimar Republic, the Russian Revolution, the coming to power of Mao in China, and the Cuban revolution. Chaotic circumstances are perfect breeding grounds for dictatorial regimes. The US constitution and the Three Branches of Government have up to now been a bulwark against this kind of scenario. The Electoral College system is already under attack.

The practice of providing bilingual government forms and the refusal of a large segment of the population of learning English, demanding all public offices provide everything in Spanish and English, has polarized and separated people from social to church activities and from the workplace, and is the root hindrance to Hispanics from attaining the American dream. Advancement in business and industry depends on the communication skills of English. Speaking English was my priority so I could participate in all that this great country had to offer.

Why in the world would you refuse to learn English and forgo opportunities?

The resistance and the encouragement from Hispanic leaders, whether it be clergy or politicians, downplaying the need to learn proper English, somehow dreaming that in the very near future Spanish will be the official language alongside English spoken in the US—this is seriously impeding the advancement of a large portion of society, and very talented and capable young people of Hispanic heritage, from advancing and gaining economic parity and benefits.

I have been in prison ministries for the better part of twenty-five years and hesitate to ask someone to read a passage out of the Bible. Hispanics are most often depending on another participant who is fluent in English and Spanish to be able to translate for them. I am myself an immigrant, arriving from Germany without any English ability, but was advised by my Jewish neighbors to enroll immediately in a high school English course, as have most other nationalities done before me who have then gained economic advancement and social status.

Obviously, there are also many Hispanic immigrants who have excellent English competency and are very successful in all areas of society, but too many are welfare recipients, and it is not due to a lack of intelligence but of priority, and therefore they are not able to advance in their fields of knowledge. I am writing this out of my sincere love for all people, regardless of origin. My mission, whether in prisons or homeless ministry, is solely for the advancement of all my brothers and sisters to gain their slice of the American dream.

A Nation Divided Cannot Stand

Abraham Lincoln and Dr. Martin Luther King spoke of Mark 3:25: "If a house is divided against itself, it cannot stand." The politically correct addressing of black people as "African American" instead of Americans has caused a divide and fueled the animosity among the American public. No black person, except an immigrant from the African continent, has ever been born in Africa. I was born in

Germany, immigrated to the United States, and became a legal citizen; I would not dream of or demand to be addressed as a German American.

We all are precious children of our Creator. My guiding light is my Lord and Savior who stated that he came to earth to seek and save the lost, and I with my last breath will emulate my Lord in any way I can and wherever there is an opportunity to fulfill this mission.

My wife and I immigrated to the US with no English language ability, only one little suitcase each, and 180.00 dollars to our name. I am forever grateful for the life this country has afforded for me and my family. My heart will always be for the people who are seeking a better life here in America. People encouraged us to attend night classes to learn English, which for the most part were comprised of immigrants themselves. Many of them were refugees fleeing Nazi Germany who in many cases had lost relatives in the Holocaust, but even though I was aware of their experience, never once have I experienced any animosity or negativity toward my wife and me. I guess they knew firsthand how important the command of English is in attaining the American dream. I feel for all people who come from a country with a different language, and I know firsthand how hard it is to learn English.

America is a nation of immigrants, and for the most part has absorbed more immigrants than any other country. America has benefitted immensely from the influx in all areas of science, innovation, art, and manufacturing, so there is a very positive side to legal immigration, but in order to be able to live in a law-abiding society, there needs to be a healthy respect for the law that protects citizens from criminal activity. With all due respect, the majority of citizens and immigrants are respecting the laws, but if we allow the watering down of the force of the law and establish sanctuary cities and states where illegal elements can safely reside without fear of being deported, then anarchy will find a very fertile ground and will in later stages wreak havoc similar to what caused the masses to seek to live here in the US.

This is not in any way anti-immigrants but a positive for immigrants so they can finally pursue their dreams in safety. Respecting and obeying the laws is an absolute necessity for this nation to remain a beacon of hope to the huddled masses.

Respect for the freedom of religion and worship of one's faith is anchored in the Constitution for good reason, for where there is no faith, there is no hope, and where there is no hope, there is lack of faith. Faith for a better future and a better life is the ingredient most necessary for a prosperous society. Faith in God augments law; obeying becomes second nature. Law-abiding citizens are the backbone of this country, far outnumbering the law-abusing members of society. Faith in a higher authority, whether it is for the government or for the God we worship, is the ingredient that allows people of all nationalities and faiths to live in harmony.

Jesus was tested for his allegiance in the time of his ministry. Mark 12:17 says, "Then Jesus said to them, 'Give back to Caesar what is Caesar's and to God what is God's.'" "Render unto Caesar" is the beginning of a phrase attributed to Jesus in the synoptic gospels, which reads in full, "Render unto Caesar the things that are Caesar's, and unto God the things that are God's" (Matthew 22:21). This phrase has become a widely quoted summary of the relationship between Christianity, secular government, and society. The original message, coming in response to a question of whether it was lawful for Jews to pay taxes to Caesar, gives rise to multiple possible interpretations about the circumstances under which it is desirable for Christians to submit to earthly authority.

If we are not obeying God, then the idea of disobeying secular authorities is easier to justify with any excuses that we can come up with. The Scriptures tell us that we cannot hide anything from God, that all will be revealed, and we all have to stand before the ultimate judge. The ultimate judge has provided us with the instructions to help us live a life worth living. There is also the teaching of what "natural law" means; individuals or society can abrogate natural law and substitute natural law with unnatural laws. They somehow find a well-thought out excuse for this new way of thinking and living in ways that lead to the disintegrating of the very stability known as the backbone of society, which is the family.

Joshua 24:14–15 says, "Now fear the Lord and serve him with all faithfulness. Throw away the gods your ancestors worshiped beyond the Euphrates River and in Egypt and serve the Lord. But if serving the Lord seems undesirable to you, then choose for yourselves this day whom you will serve, whether the gods your ancestors served beyond the Euphrates, or the gods of the Amorites, in whose land you are living. But as for me and my household, we will serve the Lord."

The gods beyond the rivers demanded the sacrifices of their children as offerings to harvest for better crop, better weather, and so on. The present offerings of babies for the sacrifice of sexual promiscuity and unfettered restrictions of sex brings with it the undoing of the natural law of creation that we cannot deny; we can murder the natural product of sexual intercourse and somehow find reasons to justify the killing of the fetuses at any state of gestation. But killing innocents is murder, and no human being with any shred of humanity in them is able to live and find rest for their souls, as their conscience will prevent their memory to ignore their deed.

Procreation means just that; it is not rocket science, it is specifically designed for the repopulation of the earth. Sex between people of the same sex is therefore against the natural order. Murdering a large portion of innocents destroys the social contract of the young, providing revenues to provide for the time when they are old, no babies, no social security. The burden on the young will increase to 55 percent of their income, as is already the case in Germany and Japan because the younger generation wants to enjoy life without the immense responsibility of raising children. Driving a Mercedes or BMW takes precedent to the burden of caring for offspring.

I frequently ask the question, would you be invited in eighteen years to the graduation party of your BMW or Mercedes? Ignoring natural laws comes at a cost, and we, just as Joshua posed the question to his people, have to decide now: who do you want to worship? But as for me and my house we will worship the Lord. This is very common sense, a very sensible plan for survival. You may call it religion. I teach the Bible for survival and a mode of overcoming whatever life throws at us, we are all born with a will to survive, and

Jesus clearly thought us, "I am the Way." To substitute his way with some other way will have completely different outcomes from what God intended for us. Jesus said, "I want you to enjoy an abundant life." Over 2.5 million people in prison can attest that a different or their way is not very enjoyable or productive; spending many years addicted or many years cooped up in a small cell does not sound very enjoyable to me.

Dr. Phil uses an expression that I borrow frequently: "How is it working out for you?" And the answer is usually, not good. The 80 percent of the millennials who are distancing themselves from a biblical worldview and religion and God are an open invitation for evil to pay them a visit, enticing them with whatsoever may work to accomplish their separation from their Creator God and fulfill the enemy's mission to kill and destroy. Evil attempted to lure Jesus to bow down to him in the desert, which tells me he stops at nothing, not even God's Son; and evil still successfully leads people to a road to destruction. Jesus warned his followers, wide is the road to destruction. In modern terms, "everybody is doing it." Yes, they are right, many are doing it and are deprived of a life worth living. St. Augustine: "If it is wrong, it is still wrong even if everybody is doing it, and right is right, even if nobody is doing it."

Considering what is now the new normal pales in comparison to anything that a person who has lived long enough and still capable of remembering considers normality, for which they are now being labeled homophobic or against whatever other unnatural activity has been legalized and considered as the new normal.

Humans cannot change natural law.

Natural law is a not just a philosophy; natural laws are certain rights, by virtue of human nature and universally recognizable through human reason. Through science or medical procedures, the LGBTQ culture has declared natural law invalid and to some extent been successful in presenting unnatural acts as a civil right now protected by law, which is still unable to prevent the psychological damage to the person who struggled with their gender identity or their desires for unnatural acts, which by themselves bring physical and psychological harm and suffering to the person.

To live an unnatural lifestyle in a natural world is by and large a feat that may only be accomplished through medical intervention and still unable to bring peace to the altered person. Rest and peace can and will only come to any human by our Creator, almost like, only a designer of a very complex machinery will be able to successfully make it possible for his creation to function properly for its intended purpose. No cultural engineering can change the natural law endowed by our Creator for the benefit of his creation.

James V. Schall said, "Things are as they are because they are created to sustain humankind. They did not bring about their own existence. We have a formal cause, a material cause, an efficient cause, and a final cause. We see that these different causes are needed to explain something real about what we encounter in the things that are. We are not gods, nor do we blend into some 'all' wherein we no longer exist in our singular identity. It is precisely the abidingness of our singular identity that is the most important thing about us. 'I' am the one who did/did not do this or that. It is that singular, unique identity by which John is not Suzie and Sally is not John, which enables us to identify the specific cause of things that come to pass in this world."

In 1988, Joseph Ratzinger recalled the famous remark of the Dutch jurist, Hugo Grotius (d. 1645), to the effect that the natural law would be the natural law "even if" God did not exist. Of this affirmation, Ratzinger remarked: "But if God does not exist, nothing will be as it is now; everything will proceed from emptiness and revert to emptiness. What we call justice will be mere caprice that we can rewrite as we will."

Things are as they are because they are created to be the way they are by a Creator. They did not bring about their own existence. "Whether or not God exists, the answer to that question will ultimately determine whether or not we are human beings, whether human dignity and true humanity and human justice can or cannot exist."

There are medical doctors and scientists who may be tempted to think that they are God; the reality is they can only think they are god! They are a great gift to the world, alleviating much suffering through the superb intellect and years and years of training that very few people would be able to undergo for many years; in some specialties requiring ten to twelve years of intense studying and financial sacrifice. But God is still God and the Creator and Lord of all. Remember the commandment "Thou shall have no other gods before me." All throughout history there were emperors, kings, and dictators who forced their people to bow down and worship them as gods, and in due time came to naught.

Reminds me of an old Austrian hymn written in 1774: "Grosser Gott Wir Loben Dich" (in English: "Holy God, We Praise Thy Name"). The first verse says, "Lord of all, we bow before thee; all on earth thy scepter claim. Infinite thy vast domain, everlasting is thy reign." It is truly hard to imagine what the future will bring when absolutes and natural laws are abolished—and replaced with what?

One only has to examine the nineteenth and twentieth century holocausts and mayhem inflicted on humanity in the East and West. Primitive and advanced nations alike who tried to create a new world order and some with the exclusion of God and the Bible, the "Basic Instructions Before Leaving Earth." We do have a life to live while on this earth, and we do need guidance from the creator designer of the body, soul, and the spirit. I surmise, that this may be the reason that the first and highest commandment is "Love the Lord with all of your heart, mind, soul, and strength," and if not, then the question arises; who and what are you offering your life to?

The ten don'ts that Moses brought down the mountain were not meant to spoil all our fun and enjoyment; they are meant so that we are able to live a life worth living. The first four deal with our relationship with God; the other six are instructions how we will be able to live with one another. Any deviance will be the beginning of strife and war even within the immediate family and the family of nations. The US Bill of Rights states it so clearly: "life, liberty, and the pursuit of happiness" is a well-known phrase in the United States Declaration of Independence. The phrase gives three examples of the unalienable rights which the Declaration says have been given to all human beings by their Creator, and which governments are created to protect.

How, then, could the US Supreme Court legalize the murder of innocents in the womb and call this barbarous procedure a woman's choice and they be the judge of the living and the dead? In the future, who else has the authority to appoint themselves judge and executioner and rename murder a choice not to be punished by law? Inconvenience should never be the deciding factor of who lives or dies.

We only have to look back eighty-one years when the Nuremberg Laws were enacted and the lives of millions of serfs, gypsies, mentally challenged, clergy, and Jews were reduced to nonhumans and exterminated by the millions, more than in all of human history, and all because a Supreme German Court bowed down to a murderous dictator who managed to order the German High Court to rob humans of their God-given dignity and influence and silence the German public by controlling the media and the police. Similarly, the Chinese Communists have empowered the young Red Guards to ostracize and shut down all opposition.

Now, here in the US, we have a similar situation carried out by students and the media, encouraged by liberal universities, colleges, professors, and teachers to shut off any speech or discussion they deem hate speech, meaning not favorable of their agenda. It is with the distinct blessing of the administrative protection that the violent students carry out their unlawful actions in hindering free speech.

Where in the world is this leading to?

If not anarchy or even the specter of a civil war, invoking the Second Amendment for carrying gun owners to make their wishes known. There is at this moment in time already a movement in Congress to abolish the Electoral College to enable the three largest states to decide elections on the plural vote and thereby destroying the small states' ability to have a voice, instead forcing them to abide and join the big states that constitute the United States. If three states rule the other forty-seven states, it will be in short order a dictatorship of those states that have managed or will manage the largest segment of welfare recipients and cater to their wishes and needs, forcing the rest of the republic to finance this new endeavor.

There are already calls to require hardworking Americans to pay reparations to any person that is dark-skinned to qualify as African

American. Explanation: so that there would be a closure for the years when America harbored slaves for labor. There is no white American alive today who personally owned slaves, and even their parents and grandparents never had anything to do with it. This movement has the potential to set the civil rights movement and race relations back, ushering in unforeseen consequences and destruction, making the casualties of the Civil War look like a small disturbance. The Civil War was fought with the purpose of abolishing slavery, and it was fought by whites fighting their brothers so that the African Americans could be free to pursue their happiness. Who could have imagined that new generations of African American would not want to depend on their own initiative to succeed?

The large number of young people from the inner cities, who are dropping out of high school and are not easily employable due to their reluctance to work in low-level entry jobs, enroll to receive benefits, be it state or US government sponsored, which are higher than their weekly paychecks would have been at their local McDonald's, and receive housing, food stamps, and heating subsidies.

Affirmative action was designed to lower the entrance examinations for college admissions, literally turning down, in some cases, qualified white and Asian students to equalize the ratios required under affirmative action. This policy will not benefit black or white or Asian, but it will create a hostile attitude, and the recipients of this benefit will not be able to compete with the students who advanced by their own drive for success.

Heather McDonald breaks this down perfectly and accurately exposes the dangers of such climates on college campuses. Heather points out the absurdity of the overwhelming numbers of liberal professors and their sanctioning of the victim mentality such as "safe spaces."

The Equal Employment Opportunity Act of 1972 is the act which gives the Equal Employment Opportunity Commission (EEOC) authority to sue in federal courts when it finds reasonable cause to believe that there has been obstruction. Equal employment opportunities are the way to achieve a better life, but ability still needs to be the determining factor in hiring and obtaining a degree.

In many cases, it is hiring by the numbers for racial equality that has resulted in a lowering of standards, which has caused the US to fall behind other industrial nations and are unable to compete in many industrial sectors.

This is where a liberal establishment is cutting off the branch they are sitting on, as the standard of living will be harder to maintain, which is already evident in the number of working hours required by a family of four where the husband and wife need both of their incomes just to keep the wolves from their door, living on a paycheck-to-paycheck basis. Large amounts of debts accumulated on credit cards and foreclosures are ample evidence of this way of life.

The ultimate question remains: How are we managing the difficulties that will arise—not *may*, but *will*—and where will we find the strength and balance in a culture that overturns natural law and forces us to move away from what the Bible has been teaching humanity for 3,000 years; that has against all obstacles made it possible to survive, thrive, and multiply; and is now in the process of being overturned and pushed out of the public square? In Scripture there is wisdom, guidance, and hope; apart from the Bible, where are our instructions for life supposed to come from? Rely on the secular civil authorities to give us direction, the same authorities who have been proven very unreliable and disastrous throughout history in many different lands and cultures? The inevitability of changing political systems and elected officials should alone be proof enough to rely on the Creator of the universe, which is big enough that we still only have minimal knowledge of the vast expanse of the solar system and its origin. Theories alone are not adequate as they have been redacted and changed numerous times in my lifetime.

The origin of the universe from a biblical understanding has not changed and has remained constant throughout the ages. Our understanding of how it revolves and operates has through science numerous times been updated, but no one knows with certainty how life began and how the universe was created except what we are told by the biblical explanation. This may sound too simple for many, but due to its infinite vastness we rely on biblical interpretation.

Chapter 17

Global Climate Change

There is a degree of disagreement in society in recent years about who is responsible and what steps are necessary to prevent the melting of the ice caps of the North Pole and the South Pole. It stretches from the bizarre to speculations and computer-generated models about the possibility of the seas rising to levels that would inundate major cities that are located near coastlines, and storms of epic proportions destroying low-lying countries, especially for a country like Bangladesh, which historically suffered floods of biblical proportions and disasters.

I am not a meteorologist or scientist, and am therefore unable to debate the issue, but what concerns me and what I am exposed to in this is the anger and hostility toward those who would even mention the possibility that it may not be caused by humans, and that mere humans are not in a position to adversely affect the climate changes that have occurred for millions and millions of years, even before the contribution of cars, coal-fired furnaces, and cows emitting too much gas into the environment. The subject is better to be avoided when in any social get-together or public square.

Lawmakers of every stripe pounce on the issue with vengeance to garner votes and then attempt to extract taxes and adherence to their laws even to the detriment of the average worker trying to feed his family. If, for any reason, anyone expresses any doubt of the scientific or political explanations, they are then labeled a deplorable ignoramus and are belittled, not just because of questioning but just of not-agreeing, therefore abrogating the very constitutional right to free speech and changing the meaning and intent to hate speech.

Instituting laws regarding what is considered hate speech approaches levels of what has occurred in Germany in the thirties enforced violently by Brownshirts. In China during the cultural revolution of the sixties and seventies, the Red Guards degraded and violently dragged anyone not in favor through the streets of their cities with baskets on their heads and sent them to reeducation camps for several years.

What has been the case at universities and colleges across America in recent years is now raised to a fever pitch with students allowed to violently prevent any opposing viewpoint, either by not permitting an invited speaker on campus or relegating them to a very small venue; and this is not because the invited speaker is inciting violence, but because a hostile segment of the student body does not want any opposing viewpoint to their agenda. Sadly, the majority of the governing bodies of these institutions are even more in tune with the students, simply because they are the very same people who have indoctrinated their pupils and therefore are the real culprits in these attacks on the constitutional rights. Instead of teaching and upholding constitutional laws, they are brazenly and openly teaching terroristic tactics, and to some degree, even participating in the acts of lawlessness.

At this moment in time in America, it is not advisable for anyone to express or share their opinion. How is it possible that this is even happening in the country known as the land of the free and the brave? The hostility encountered in the family, workplace, and church is responsible for small talk; guests are advised not to touch on subjects to which someone in the family or guests might object. No lively discussion is possible and many reach for their cell phones.

I am by nature inquisitive and many times make statements to gather people's opinion on any given subject which in the past has brought out many different viewpoints that I was privileged to learn from. This has now become a dangerous exercise in futility due to the hostility displayed almost without fail. The Political Correctness Syndrome mentality has now reached the height of a terroristic nature where mob-like behavior is encouraged by certain political interests taking advantage of the socialistic teachings of high school, and college teachers who seem to have missed history classes and are not very educated of the socialistic movement's catastrophic consequences.

I am not suggesting ignorance here; no, what I am pointing to is a deliberate social agenda of a new world order that is advocating the impoverishment of the workers in the advanced west to transfer their hard-earned wealth and knowledge and distribute it among the underdeveloped world to accommodate their liberalism learnt in high school and college. Many of the students and faculties never have experienced the corruption and dictatorial conditions in those supposedly utopian socialist countries. Asian countries like China and the African continent are riddled with graft, corruption, and violence for anyone raising their voices, the likes of which have not been displayed since the violent Middle Ages.

Genocides are perpetrated and repeated in many countries and will continue to be repeated if western nations are transferring huge amounts of money into the hands of their corrupt government officials. So, the distribution of wealth has been a disaster for the poor and has raised a whole new crop of corrupt officials who enrich themselves, transfer development funds to their own private accounts, and are more than willing to silence any opposition.

The warring factions are responsible for the destruction of farmland in the African nations due to the expropriation of farms from their rightful owners, who happen to be experienced farmers; the indiscriminate killing of the very people who worked those farms and the killing of their livestock is reminiscent of the Crusades, where the supply chain of the advancing troops outstripped the capacity to nourish and replenish, and the expropriation of food became a necessity for them to sustain the Crusade. This then brought suffering to the very people they tried to save from the Islamic hordes.

This is seen repeatedly in many nations, followed with the calls from the UN for large amounts of food supplies to avoid human catastrophes for millions who are near starvation. The UN is constantly haranguing western nations for their human rights violations, but completely ignoring the fact that these disasters are caused by their own leadership.

The indoctrination of the student bodies is showing results of an unimaginable magnitude displayed in the American higher education institutions. The emergence of extreme radical left Congressional aspirants, many very successfully entering the halls of Congress, should be proof to anyone following the radical news media controlled by their foreign benefactors, the chief instigators of this agenda.

How the very intelligent young people can be so easily be misled, and be unaware that the very same contributors have garnered their wealth in most cases from these poor countries, which are unable to defend themselves against the corporate raiders, currency manipulators, and their power, which made it possible for them to continue their exploitations of a poor country's mineral wealth.

America is a land of opportunities due to its free press, a constitutionally protected juridicial system, and the separation of power by the three branches of government. Yes, we are very fortunate to be the beneficiaries of very wise founders who knew the shortcomings of the European types of governments and their kings. Why attempt to destroy the only democracy in this world that has lasted more than three hundred years and produced a standard of living for 320 million people far beyond any nation, especially considering the diversity of people coming together without the constant threat of civil war and destruction?

There are forces at work in the US that are constantly trying to pit black against white and Hispanic against white by way of demanding Spanish as a second language in public offices. All that this is accomplishing, as commerce is conducted in English, is that those who are not fluent in English are cheating themselves and experience disadvantages.

This has created division and separation, which was experienced by all new arrivals for a time. It has always been present in America, with one significant difference: all the other immigrants without fail have assimilated and used their command of English to advance in commerce and education and rely less on government assistance. This is in no way intended to degrade any one ethnicity or race; I am only speaking from my own experience and that of my friends who all came to America without any English ability. They made it their number one priority to learn the language so they were able to take advantage of every opportunity that presented itself but were attainable only through the ability to read contracts and negotiate and facilitate business deals.

I have in my lifetime in America been acquainted with people of all races who became very successful in their businesses because of their command of English. I am stressing this to the point of screaming, so that my black and Hispanic brothers and sisters and any other minority will hear it, so that they also will partake of all the opportunities that are available to anyone willing to invest their energy and aspirations in their pursuit of the American dream, which is alive and well, as demonstrated by the success of people coming from all corners of the world. They are contributing to the unparalleled economic success of the US, which is envied by people of other nations and the reason for the large numbers of people trying to enter the US legally.

Sadly, you have now a very large number of immigrants crashing the gates without adhering to the legality of their entries, and this will inevitably lead to more of a divide and division.

Which brings me back to where I started, about the need of a moral and ethical standard that is necessary to sustain the life of the population, regardless of creed or color, and the need to uphold the constitutional right of all people. This is a very sticky issue that is not compatible with the Muslims worshipping the Islamic faith, and due to the Quran's demands, a devout adherent cannot follow a democratic government that provides equal protection and rights to any male or female.

A good example is the New Testament Scripture in Mark 12:1, mentioned earlier. Jesus, when asked about the one whom they shall serve, took a coin and asked, "Whose picture is on the coin?" It was Caesar's. He instructed them to give to Caesar what belongs to Caesar and give to God what belongs to God. That is true today as it was two thousand years ago. We cannot serve two masters, and this is not feasible by being a devout Muslim and asked to follow US law above the Quran in public or family life.

That may be the main issue and reason that no Islamic nation resembles any kind of democracy. The Tunisian French-language poet Abdelwahab Meddeb wrote *The Malady of Islam*, a book that points out the radicalization of the Islamic youth by television news and TV shows and now the Internet, opening their eyes to the living standards of the western societies. Students are then being incited by the Muslim clerics that the reason for their lack of wealth is because they must have been robbed, never admitting their shortcomings in advanced education and science and commerce due to their higher educational institutions' teaching methods and ways of life that are based in the seventh century. In the twelfth and fourteenth century, Islamic science was on par with western science and advanced technology for that time, and then came a regression, and Islamic nations have never recovered.

Islam taught the western world, and for whatever reason it stalled after the defeat by the Spanish in Spain and they were forced to retreat. The attempt to take over Europe also came to a halt when the combined Austrian and Polish forces stopped the Islamic armies' advance at the doors of Vienna and forced them to retreat back across the Bosporus, to present-day Turkey.

After the Ottoman Empire was replaced by the British in 1919, they languished until Atta Turk reestablished present-day Turkey. Kemal Ataturk, soldier, statesman, and reformer, was the founder and first president (1923–38) of the Republic of Turkey. He modernized the country's legal and educational systems and encouraged the adoption of a European way of life, with a Latin alphabet and citizens adopting European-style names. This has not been repeated in any other Islamic country.

Now we are witnessing the systematic unraveling in modern-day Turkey by the Muslim Brotherhood, which is actively pursuing to recreate the caliphate in the Middle East, with disastrous results, leading to the deaths of hundreds of thousands of Christians and the killing of their own Shiite or Sunni brothers and sisters. The destruction is unimaginable, with the suffering of their people living under constant wars. Saudi Wahabism delegates and enforces strict Sharia laws, the hacking off of limbs and the caning of women for not adhering to Islamic dress codes and being subjugated by their own husbands. These rules are the main culprit for their third world economic development, creating the insufficiency of their rulers to provide employment for the young and little hope for economic advancements, instead relying on oil revenues, which necessitates western technologies and workers to maintain and operate.

Christianity has provided the engines for the emergence of commerce and industrialization, making it possible at times to feed the rest of the world and supply the world with the know-how necessary to alleviate suffering through medicine, technology, and advanced agriculture. The Spanish Inquisition has often been named the major failure of Christianity. The Inquisition was established in the fifteenth century and was criticized for failing to act like Christians. But this completely ignores the persecutions of Christians in the nineteenth and twentieth centuries in every Islamic country, with maybe one or two exceptions, Egypt and Tunisia. The Western Christian nations have allowed mosques to be built, with maybe a few exceptions, and tolerated, and not persecuted, Muslims. There are numerous Islamic nations who are preventing Christians from government employments and free enterprise.

You can just imagine what the situation will be when western nations, due to the influx of Muslim immigration, adhere to the teachings of the Quran, which specifically disallows Muslims from becoming friendly with non-Muslims, and what the consequences this will have on commerce and trade within each country. The hostility and separation between citizens may bring the reintroduction of civil strife, reminiscent of the Middle Ages.

There should be no ill will between religions, whether it be Islam, Hinduism, Buddhism, or any other, with the understanding that human rights law supersedes all religious law regardless of their teachings. Traditions and customs are important, and they can be practiced in different nations, as long as they conform with the laws of the land. The US is in many ways an oddity among nations as the US Constitution guarantees religious freedom for all, but not any religious laws to be imposed on the people of other faiths. Germany has been under the power of the clerical influence, and in some

German States, still is. The National Church of England is today the Anglican Church with considerable power over the English public. Each of the previous mentioned nations are governed by and under democratic constitutions.

The US had for many years been influenced by Protestantism and to an extend by the Catholic Church which has enabled the US to flourish among nations to a position of world dominance and in some cases has even abused this power and exploited other nations. The US Constitution is the cornerstone that guarantees people to live their faith under the umbrella of unity and equality; what I mean by that is, no one entity or religion can impose their practices on someone else, and the practices have to be within what the law allows. Islam seems to have the most difficulty with this concept, as the Quran explicitly forbids the befriending and the assimilation of Muslims with Christians, unbelievers.

The Quran says, "O you who believe! do not take the Jews and the Christians for friends; they are friends of each other; and whoever amongst you takes them for a friend, then surely he is one of them; surely Allah does not guide the unjust people" (5:51).

Q5:57 says, "Believers! Do not seek the friendship of those who were given the Book before you or the disbelievers who ridicule your religion and make a jest of it. Have a fear of God, if you are true Muslims believers who befriend unbelievers will abide in hell."

Q5:80 says, "You see many among them making friends with unbelievers. Evil is that to which their souls prompt them. They have incurred the wrath of God and shall endure eternal torment."

Q3:118 says, "Believers, do not make friends (Pagans, Jews, Christians, Hypocrites) with any but your own people. Others will spare no pains to corrupt you. They desire nothing but your ruin. Their hatred is evident from what they utter with their mouths, but greater is the hatred which their breasts conceal. We have made plain to you Our revelations. Strive to understand them. Don't befriend infidels except for protecting yourself… And for this reason they pose a threat to the unity amongst the populace and rightly so, as their Holy Book makes it very difficult to accommodate unbelievers and be friends with them."

Chapter 18

Legal Immigration

America is by far the most diverse country in the world, with people from just about every race and creed intermarried. Everyone has been the beneficiary of all kinds of different foods, customs, talents, and ingenuity. The last names of the inventors registered in the US Patent office speak volumes of people from all over the world contributing to the American dream.

Even with all this, one might think that this would be a shining example what humanity can accomplish when there is harmony, and yet there is a troubling trend: Islam, which cannot and will not, with a few exceptions, assimilate into the American culture. The understanding of the responsibility of an immigrant coming to America was probably never better stated than by Theodore Roosevelt, who said in 1907 that immigrants should assimilate and become "loyal Americans":

> In the first place, we should insist that if the immigrant who comes here in good faith becomes an American and assimilates himself to us, he shall be treated on an exact equality with everyone else, for it is an outrage to discriminate against any such man because of creed, or birthplace, or origin. But this is predicated upon the person's becoming in every facet an American, and nothing but an American. There can be no divided allegiance here. Any man who says he is

an American, but something else also, isn't an American at all. We have room for but one flag, the American flag. We have room for but one language here, and that is the English language. And we have room for but one sole loyalty and that is a loyalty to the American people.

The Congress's responsibility is to ensure in legislation and laws that cannot be watered down to gain political advantage by allowing preference to a certain ethnicity to not learn English and forcing the rest of the population to accept a foreign language to be the official second language on all official documents and tests. This alone will ensure continued animosity between people of different origins who have never demanded or been given this privilege. As President Roosevelt stated, "We have room for only one official language," and that is not to disadvantage a certain people but to ensure that they too are able to gain economic power and wealth.

I am a German immigrant, and I recall the difficulty the English language presented to me. It compelled me to attend high school at night and become proficient enough to be successful in business. I cannot even imagine the difficulty of people from countries with different alphabets and symbols. But the fact that their children excel in high schools and colleges is proof enough that anyone can attain a degree of sufficiency to succeed and not depend on government assistance, which is often offered by politicians who are more concerned about their reelection than the welfare of their constituents.

Immigrants without the ability to read or write or speak English, are at a disadvantage in the workplace and society. No one should abandon their native mother language, but the reality is, in the workplace and the business world, it is of utmost importance to attain a certain level of proficiency in English to be a contributor and not a liability to society.

Puerto Rico is a part of the US and are American citizens able to enter the US without restrictions. Puerto Rico has Spanish as the official language and no need to learn English to succeed in Puerto Rico, but when relocating to the mainland, English is necessary in negotiating contracts and signing paperwork where people not fluent in English are easily taken advantage of. Reading English and writing English is the foundation of success, and it cannot be overstated enough.

I know, it is not politically correct, but the reality is that is what goes through people's mind. I want everyone to succeed regardless of color, creed, or ethnicity. Not to be politically correct can easily be construed as racist, or anti-something, whatever may be the mantra of the time. But how can you love people and not speak the truth, which necessitates lying to their faces and encouraging people to continue on the road they are traveling on, regardless of the harm it causes in their future?

Erwin Lutzer wrote, and I paraphrase: "If you tell people what they want to hear, you will have a large audience. If you tell them what they need to hear, you will have a small audience. But I think if you don't tell them what they need to hear, than you are not their friend." That basically is what the Gospel proclaims; if you want to save your life, you have to lose it. Jesus for sure was not politically correct when he walked this earth, and the result was, that they soon took him out of it.

Chapter 19

Political Correctness

In the times we live in now, we are experiencing a new phenomenon; if someone speaks the truth, he or she will be destroyed by accusations of something they may have said twenty or thirty years ago. Or if the person was alone with someone of the opposite sex in a room alone, they are accused of touching them inappropriately.

Ample evidence of this travesty was exposed when Judge Cavanaugh was before the Senate Panel and a lady professor came forward and gave testimony about a frat party they both supposedly attended thirty-two years ago, and stated that she was drunk enough not to remember being there, and a year later, after the hearings, admits that it was all made up. The political correctness police engages the media to enforce and convict and destroy careers in the public forum and anyone who opposes their liberal agenda.

Paula Dean, who admitted before a Federal Grand Jury that she used a racial slur twenty-five years earlier, was driven off her very successful cooking show, as one advertiser after another withdrew their commercials. These are not isolated instances; they are very popular in political circles as well as in the media. Judge Roy Moore from Alabama lost his Senate bid, due to the last-minute accusations made by the political opponent. Is this really the world we want to live in? A powerful lobby or media can obstruct and reconstruct the Constitution, the Bill of Rights, and natural law according to their agenda.

The term *hate speech* is likened to screaming "fire" in movie theatres for what hate speech can cause. This has not a scintilla of similarity with the First Amendment concept of free speech. An opinion expressed is not a movie house scream; it simply means that I do not have to agree with someone, and they do not have to agree with me. We should be able to agree to disagree. Tolerance is only tolerant when we listen to someone else's opinion. This is at this time in our culture not possible, as it is deleted or shouted down so no one will be able to hear an objective opinion other than our own preconceived opinion.

The scenario is already on display in the refusal to accept an election by the Constitutional Electoral College System guaranteeing small states may not be shut out by votes from the most populated states. Los Angeles alone would have more power over who gets elected than forty-three states of the Union. Two years of concoction of collusion and interference by a two-bit dictator, hamstringing our democracy of any legislative activity and all energy expended to the removal of a duly elected president. For two years now, the American people are not benefiting from those they have elected, a hundred days of no progress is certainly not what the electorate had in mind.

With all that is changing in the political landscape, and the secular cultural changes that have been embraced by a large percentage of the millennial and the older liberal establishment, what's left for the rest of the population who have not abandoned biblical truths for a no-absolute truth culture? The new culture is teaching the overwhelming philosophical agenda in schools and academia, and now inundates the new political newcomers who are not favorable to a conservative viewpoint, with a viewpoint that you deserve it, you do not have to earn it, and it can be disappropriated from the rich and handed over to those less inclined to the idea of hard work and living within their means. This has the unmistakable aroma of a regime that operates more like the teaching of Karl Marx than of Dale Carnegie.

The economic model of the US is not by any means the only successful and politically correct model to follow. There are other nations, especially some Northern European nations, who are more like semi-socialistic nations where the lower classes are provided free healthcare which is paid for by the collection of taxes and the general fund. In the case of Norway, it is oil revenues from the North Sea oil rigs. Germany is funding its healthcare system through the collection of very high contributions from the payroll tax.

One of the side effects of a social medical and social welfare system is the disintegration of faith-based beliefs and reliance on God for the health of the heart and the soul. The "cradle to the grave" social reliance has caused the abandonment of church attendance and the necessity of spiritual health and faith in the existence of God.

In recent articles in a political magazine, the question was posed: Why are people not attending church anymore? In a recent poll, the overriding answers where 90 percent negative, with comments ranging from labeling religion "hocus pocus" or "fairytales," to evolutionary theory rendering Christianity obsolete and irrelevant in a modern society. Some comments were even using comedy to explain why people still cling to their faith, or belittled people and declared them deplorables who do not know any better, ignoring three thousand years of Jewish history and two thousand years of Christianity and the moral compass and ethical teaching and the hope it has brought to people through the ages in their most difficult times and personal tragedies.

When hearts are broken and hope evaporates due to circumstances beyond our control, question is, where do we turn to? Does any government program soothe a broken heart or bring hope to someone in need of strength beyond their condition?

Chapter 20

Christian Unity

John 6:68 tells us how people in all the ages have questioned the value of belief in Jesus Christ and his redeeming power. John 6:51–68 (NIV) says,

> "I am the living bread that came down from heaven. Whoever eats this bread will live forever. This bread is my flesh, which I will give for the life of the world."
>
> Then the Jews began to argue sharply among themselves, "How can this man give us his flesh to eat?"
>
> Jesus said to them, "Very truly I tell you, unless you eat the flesh of the Son of Man and drink his blood, you have no life in you. Whoever eats my flesh and drinks my blood has eternal life, and I will raise them up at the last day. For my flesh is real food and my blood is real drink. Whoever eats my flesh and drinks my blood remains in me, and I in them. Just as the living Father sent me and I live because of the Father, so the one who feeds on me will live because of me. This is the bread that came down from heaven."
>
> On hearing it, many of his disciples said, "This is a hard teaching. Who can accept it?"

> Aware that his disciples were grumbling about this, Jesus said to them, "Does this offend you? Yet there are some of you who do not believe." From this time many of his disciples turned back and no longer followed him. "You do not want to leave too, do you?" Jesus asked the Twelve. Simon Peter answered him, "Lord, to whom shall we go? You have the words of eternal life."

This brings up again the question to whom, to where, and to what will we turn, and what will it look like and how will it nourish not only our bodies but our hearts and souls?

This passage of Scripture has been debated for two thousand years. Is Jesus present in the transubstantiation or only present in the Spirit or not at all and reduced to something that occurred two thousand years ago that we should only remember?

In the Catholic faith, it is the miracle of the wine and the bread as the actual presence of Jesus's body and blood that we partake in the Eucharistic Communion necessary for us to be able to overcome the trials of life that come our way. In the Protestant tradition, some denominations acknowledge the Spiritual presence of the Lord in the Communion, and some teach that preaching and reading of the Bible is enough for spiritual nourishment and survival.

Denying the need for spiritual nourishment and Christian fellowship leaves the door open for all kinds of attachments to the ever-changing ways of the culture. Some of them are very harmful and in many cases are leading to dependency of alcohol and drugs, and even to mental breakdowns. I have for the last eight years ministered to mental patients in mental institutions and am acutely aware of the consequences of people who have lost contact and fellowship with either their family or faith and drifted toward desperation and overwhelming loneliness.

There are many mental sicknesses in need of medical treatment or psychiatric treatment, but my experience has been that even medical personal has recommended pastoral care and the conducting of church services in the dormitories of the mental facilities. I can only speak from my own experiences of the positive impact these services have on the patients. Prison ministry has shown similar improvements in the behavior and attitudes of the inmate population and is now welcomed and encouraged by staff and administration.

The spiritual departments in hospitals have for many patients been a lifeline of hope and strength to overcome their predicament, and in many cases, requested repeatedly for spiritual care. For me, I can only attest what I experience once a week as I go from room to room and ask, after introducing myself as a spiritual care volunteer, if they would like a prayer or receive Holy Communion, and in the majority of cases I am invited to pray with them and administer communion.

There are patients who when admitted declare themselves as NOR, NONE, Atheist, DNS, Catholic, or any of the myriad Evangelical Denominations. Surprisingly enough, many who are not devout Catholics or Protestants are inclined and very open to prayer for healing and restoration. And there are patients who adamantly resist any spiritual care, but are open to just a friendly visit; I guess just a need to speak to someone neutral, and these situations have been a real uplift for my volunteer work in pastoral care.

I have shared in meetings for new prison minister volunteers that the human contact from one person to another is of monumental importance for the dignity and humanity that someone is caring enough to give of themselves to the least of these, as Jesus taught us. It was the presence of Jesus that the lepers, the cripples, the deaf and the blind were aware of when they called out to him to be made well. They did not place their hopes and recovery into their ruling powers, but in the Son of Man, who came to seek and save the lost. Again quoting Teresa of Avila, "You and I are the hands and feet of Jesus on this earth." I am convinced that the millennial generation is encouraged not adverse to be part of outreach in their communities and will be sharing their talents and energies to bind up the wounds of the brokenhearted. I am sure they will find what they are missing in their lives.

Christianity has for two thousand years been the engine that drove charity through institutions and hospitals and missions in every country on earth and it is still the largest charitable organization today. It was born out of the teaching of Jesus Christ and is bearing fruit throughout the world.

Chapter 21

World Religions

Hinduism, probably the oldest religion, where Buddhism has its origin, is beset even to this day with the caste system, relegating certain humans to be untouchables, with no hope of overcoming their plight of living as a lower class. A caste system is a class structure that is determined by birth. Loosely, it means that in some societies, if your parents are poor, you're going to be poor, too. Same goes for being rich. Hinduism is the oldest religion on the planet earth to my knowledge.

Buddhism as it is practiced in China has kept the masses in dire circumstances, being manipulated by emperors for centuries and then by communist dictators, and at the present is still in the clutches of communism and persecuting Christians to the point of death. To confess to be a Christian in China today is very dangerous, because of Jesus's statement: "I am the way and the truth, and the truth will set you free." Well, that does not sit well with dictators, and especially Communist societies where freedom is anathema to Communist rule. Bibles are strictly forbidden, and assemblies of worshippers are labeled as an insurrectionist activity; people are sent to reeducation or labor camps.

Islamic nations are not by any stretch of the imagination resembling democracies where there is equality of man and woman. Worshipping Christ or any other religion in some Islamic countries is an offense against Allah and still punishable by beheading or by stoning to death.

Can any of these religious systems be transplanted into western democracies? I argue not, since there is no credible evidence in the world to point to where Christians are not persecuted or harassed. Egypt and Jordan may qualify, but recent persecution and killing of Coptic Christians in Egypt has taken a heavy toll. Christian churches have been burned and Christians murdered in many African nations and in India and Islamic nations where extremists harm Christians and are tolerated by their governments.

How, then, can it be explained that an educated millennial generation has abandoned the faith of Christianity to follow a postmodern belief that life is possible without absolute truths; that they actively seek to transform a way of life that has raised the standard of living to an unimaginable level sought after by millions of people, causing them to abandon their homeland and try to enter the US, legally or illegally, by the millions every year? Would not those statistics alone convince the postmodern liberal establishment to reconsider their stance on Christianity and American democracy?

Any nation has a duty to care for their own first and foremost; it is stated and professed in the swearing in of the president and it has nothing to do with racism, it has all to do with self-preservation. A nation without secure borders and without immigration laws is not a nation.

This can also be applied to natural law and spiritual law; the Ten Commandments were not given to us to spoil our fun but to enable us to live in a world that has respect for our fellow human beings and for God, or, as it is now interpreted, a higher power, whatever that may be or include. "Thou shall have no other gods but me." The God of the Bible does not share his glory with any other gods, regardless of who else we decide to worship.

Six commandments deal with our relationship with our human travelers, and lo and behold, many of our civil laws are based on biblical laws. Thou shalt not murder, steal, covet, give false witness, or commit adultery; thou shalt honor your father and mother. Well, every one of these is necessary for a civil society; without it would be like playing football without any rules. Within a short time there would be nobody left on the playing field well enough to play. In evolutionary teaching, the bigger fish eat the smaller fish; empathy and compassion and caring for the weak is not part of the animal world.

If we continue to relegate faith and reason to the backwaters of the public square, the logical sequence will be an evolutionary animalistic society. As far as I know, there are no gifts of the Holy Spirit shared in the animal world. Galatians 5:22–23 says, "But the fruit of the Spirit is love, joy, peace, forbearance, kindness, goodness, faithfulness, gentleness, and self-control." In the absence of these gifts, what kind of existence will that portend? Not everyone alive adheres and practices these gifts, but Christian teaching has always encouraged people to embody these gifts to the best of their ability.

Chapter 22

Darwinism, Marxism, Socialism

History provides ample evidence of how the absence of a moral compass and lack of compassion can lead to atrocities of unimaginable dimensions. Russia is a prime example, with the destruction of 50,000 churches and the murder of 50,000 priests and ministers in the years following the ascent of an atheistic ruling party that governed the Soviet Union from 1917 until 1989. The murder of 20 million of their own citizens and the destruction of free enterprise, which was forcibly converted to a socialistic economic system that stifled entrepreneurial opportunities, reduced Russia to a third world nation, unable to feed its own people. China fared no better; neither did any other atheistic country that was and still is ruled by Marxist ideology. The human spirit does not prosper or reinvent or lend itself to that kind of way of life.

Free enterprise, for all its shortcomings, has brought advances in industry, science, medicine, communication. There seems to be a resurgence of politicians who are eager to put severe limitations on the economy in the name of averting climate change; that is the vehicle used to accomplish their goal of severely hamstringing industry, whether it is coal, oil, automobiles, or agriculture. This will have the effect of millions of Americans having to rely on government subsidies and handouts, and they will vote for those who control the necessities for their sustenance. Cuba and Venezuela are glaring examples of the results of such political system. These are countries with enough wealth in minerals, oil, human capital, and entrepreneurial spirit that, if unleashed, that could feed and prosper the populace. (And it did so before communism was introduced.) It was capable of providing the masses with a reasonable standard of living.

In the 1800s, there was Karl Marx (1818–1883) who called religion opium for the poor suffering workers, convincing the people that Communism, a classless society, would be better than religion; no God and no religion, everybody in the same boat. Only the leaders living in splendor and deciding who is to live or die, building on Charles Darwin's *Origin of Species*, a scientific viable mechanism of natural selection, or, as it became known, "the survival of the fittest." Friedrich Nietzsche (1844–1900) rejected Christianity, calling it the religion of the weak, a slave morality. He prophesied the age of *Ubermensch*, the "Superhuman."

Adolf Hitler, convinced that the Aryan race would be the natural super race, declared all others *Untermensch*, meaning "slave laborers," and when these were exhausted and unable to contribute to society, these unproductive members of society would be eliminated by whatever means. Auschwitz was the next step. This was the progression that ensued following the teachings of Marx, Nietzsche, and Margret Sanger.

In America, eugenics was instituted and propagated by Margret Sanger, sterilizing the undesirables, zeroing in on the poor black population giving birth to too many black babies who were destabilizing society.

Karl Marx did have a point; maybe not in the way he imagined it, but nevertheless, religion has been a soothing medicine throughout the ages. The rich and the poor have overcome all kinds of calamities and disasters and wars through faith.

My view is this: Even as Rome and the popes have many times proven their ineptness and not been a shining example of Christianity, with popes failing miserably as the "Vicar of Christ," it is also true that they have in every century since Jesus walked this earth resisted the powers of their days. Maybe not as perfect as in Monday morning quarterbacking eyes seen in our day, but the Roman Catholic Church has been a bulwark against the Powers of Evil, as President Reagan named them, mainly the Soviet Union among those who publicly proclaimed that there will be no more religion to speak of. After all, as Joseph Stalin stated, "How many Soldiers does the Pope have?"

The story is told that when Emperor Napoleon took Pope Vincent XI captive and pronounced that he would destroy the Catholic faith, Pope Vincent laughed at him and said: "We have been trying to despoil the church already 1,800 years and been very unsuccessful." Matthew 16:18 says, "And I tell you that you are Peter, and on this rock I will build my church, and the gates of Hades will not overcome it."

Over three millenniums, there were numerous evil rulers and kings who aspired to be a god. We can even go back to the Book of Daniel 4:33–37 for evidence of this:

> Immediately what had been said about Nebuchadnezzar was fulfilled. He was driven away from people and ate grass like the ox. His body was drenched with the dew of heaven until his hair grew like the feathers of an eagle and his nails like the claws of a bird. At the end of that time, I, Nebuchadnezzar, raised my eyes toward heaven, and my sanity was restored.
>
> Then I praised the Most High, I honored and glorified him who lives forever. His dominion is an eternal dominion; his kingdom endures from generation to generation. All the peoples of the earth are regarded as nothing. He does as he pleases with the powers of heaven and the peoples of the earth. No one can hold back his hand or say to him: "What have you done?"
>
> At the same time that my sanity was restored, my honor and splendor were returned to me for the glory of my kingdom. My advisers and nobles sought me out, and I was restored to my throne and became even greater than before.
>
> Now I, Nebuchadnezzar, praise and exalt and glorify the King of heaven, because every-

thing he does is right, and all his ways are just. And those who walk in pride he is able to humble.

The kings that succeeded Nebuchadnezzar did not learn much: Daniel 11:36–39 tells us of King Cyrus, who said:

> Then the king shall do according to his own will: he shall exalt and magnify himself above every god, shall speak blasphemies against the God of gods, and shall prosper till the wrath has been accomplished; for what has been determined shall be done. He shall regard neither the God of his fathers nor the desire of women, nor regard any god; for he shall exalt himself above them all. But in their place, he shall honor a god of fortresses; and a god which his fathers did not know he shall honor with gold and silver, with precious stones and pleasant things. Thus he shall act against the strongest fortresses with a foreign god, which he shall acknowledge, and advance its glory; and he shall cause them to rule over many and divide the land for gain.

That was King Cyrus speaking.

In the Middle Ages, the kings in Italy, France, Germany, and Austria all wanted to be a supreme being and decide what faith and which faith will be state religion, and to some degree they did succeed, but not for long.

Matthew 16:18 says, "And I tell you that you are Peter, and on this rock, I will build my church, and the gates of Hades will not overcome it." The New Living Translation renders it as, "Now I say to you that you are Peter (which means 'rock'), and upon this rock I will build my church, and all the powers of hell will not conquer it." The Catholic Church interprets this passage as the church that Jesus was talking about; the Protestant church interprets this passage differently as referring to the Body of Christ, meaning all Christ-believing congregations.

When the apostle John the Evangelist wrote the Book of Revelation while in exile on the Island of Patmos, Nero was the ruler of Rome. The Christian churches in Asia Minor and the underground church were suffering terribly and it seemed that all hope was lost. But not so, John wrote Revelation to remind the people of the Way, that God was and is the one who will prevail against all odds. When the "Hallelujah Chorus" is performed, every person attending the performance stands up; people realize, at the end of the day of their life, everyone has to stand before God, and every knee shall bow before the Lord.

The Catholic Church was the church Jesus built and has prevailed for 2,000 years. Was it ever perfect? No, it was ruled by human beings under the protection of God. Remember the Martin Luther hymn: "A Mighty Fortress Is Our God," and the power of evil will not overcome. It may seem weak for a time, but never overcome. Governors who signed legislation, permitting abortion up to birth, or the former president, who declared that America is not a Christian Nation will not prevail.

The postmodern worldview will inevitably self-destruct as it is unable to police the hordes who will control life in the cities and fan out to the counties as it is already in evident in the proliferation of the drug trade and crime organizations too powerful for local sheriff departments for lack of funds and resources. The uncontrolled influx of illegal immigrants protected by sanctuary cities and states allowing these elements to go on unencumbered by federal agents. I wish I could blame this all on some senile illusion, but is already too real across the country and can and should wake up the generation I am devoting this book to. Quoting President Reagan again: "If we ever forget that we are One Nation Under God, then we will be a nation gone under."

Chapter 23

The Power of Faith

Faith plays a large role in how people respond to economic malaises, or natural disasters, or the destructions that wars have brought on nations and their peoples. The hope for a better life for themselves and their children has brought many nations back from war-induced destruction and despair. Without question, there is no limit to what the human spirit can accomplish when given the freedom to engage in their desire to create a better life.

I have experienced the rebirth of a nation from utter destruction that never before in history was heaved on a country. I was born in 1943 when the shadows of defeat became evident and the German government was exacting unimaginable sacrifices from their population. There was the relentless bombing of German industries and cities by American and British bombers, reducing them to rubble. There were untold civilian casualties unable to escape the destruction of their homes. Millions of fathers were in POW camps, some for up to ten years in Russia, with 90 percent never returning to their families. Fourteen million people of German descent were evicted from their ancestral homes due to the decree at the Potsdam Conference legalizing the expulsion, causing the revenge killing of 3 million people on their trek to Germany proper and never accounted for.

I am not laying any blame on the victorious Allies or on the countries who followed the decree of expulsion, but just imagine 11 million refugees flooding into what remained of Germany and immediately starting the rebuilding of their homeland. I remember, as a child, the people attending the Masses on Sundays. It got to the point that you needed to be there early to gather a seat in the pews. Saturdays were spent going to Confession in order to be able to receive the Eucharist.

Faith was taken very seriously and practiced regularly, and I would venture that it was precisely faith that allowed Germany to recover from WWII in the fifteen years following the Armistice in 1945 signaling its end.

Faith in the God of Abraham, Isaac, and Jacob, and in the Resurrection of Jesus Christ, provided the hope and the guidance to love our neighbors, whoever they were and from wherever they came from, making the remarkable recovery possible. In the postmodern society in which we now live, morals and ethics are not gleaned from the Bible but from the ideology and teaching of evolution, a worldview without any absolute truths, and where all laws are subject to the prevailing feelings of the majority, or even of the minority of the courts rendering natural laws obsolete and instituting unnatural laws and lifestyles that are to be worshipped, and, if necessary, enforced upon those who for moral reasons object and refuse to bow down to the new order.

The disintegration of the moral order has serious consequences, as a society needs moral laws not just to function but more also to survive. Somebody coined the phrase, "Laws are made to be broken." Human beings are direct descendants of Adam and Eve, who were told not to eat the apple from the tree of knowledge of good and evil, and yet they did. The story is as old as the Bible, but it also teaches us, that we are not to take the laws into our own hands, that there is someone greater than we are, and since he is the Creator and not the created, we fall into the trap to worship what we created and not the Creator.

This is in essence is the overriding calamity that we are experiencing in this moment in time, and it is not the first time. The ancient Hebrews and all the empires that have followed all worshipped their pagan gods and collapsed under the weight of immorality and greed. To worship the Creator and not the created is of utmost importance for the survival of a nation and the society within them. If you compare the life of any nation to any game that is played as a national sport, there are rules and regulations that are necessary for the safety of the players. Traffic on the nation's highways is regulated to a very high degree to assure safe travel for people who need to get to work or are enjoying a Sunday drive with their families. There are always people who disobey the rules, just as Adam and Eve, but disobeying laws always brings consequences and negative outcomes.

Self-Preservation

There is no limit to human ingenuity, as has been demonstrated throughout history over and over, from the invention of the wheel to the space race and the ensuing explosion of the Internet and the capabilities of a handheld telephone, able to speak to someone on the other side of the globe, but there is a limit to human mental capacity and endurance and stamina when the soul of a human being is stretched wider and further through the expectations of their spouses, family, work, or financial difficulties related to a living standard that is above the ability of the breadwinners to sustain, which produces anxieties beyond their capabilities to cope.

We now observe the consumption of anxiety-reducing drugs; overuse of alcoholic beverages, which may lead to DUIs and even more stress; the dependency and addiction of opioids or cannabis to provide a moment of escape from the mounting burdens that seem to be unmanageable and the desperate need to find relief from the malaise besetting this poor soul.

There is an absence of a spiritual life, or the presence of one that is practiced only occasionally when the major Christian holidays approach, limited to a yearly participation in attending a Mass or attending other Christian denominational services where the Good News is preached. The American family has undergone tremendous changes over the last fifty years, family members spreading out all across the country for job opportunities, more favorable climates, and differences of cost of living in different regions. It is in many cases not the close-knit living in near proximity to their closest relatives as was the case years ago. There is no church to provide an extended family when one's own is too far away and unable to help when aid is needed.

Turning to a Church Family in a Time of Need

Barring a church family in time of need, where do people turn to?

The option most likely is some form of government assistance, federal or state, in the form of food stamps, housing assistance, heating, medical aid. In whatever form it is received and how necessary it is to survive, there is the reality of human nature to become dependent and addicted to the lure of not having the need to get enough sleep, or to rise early in the morning to be able to leave the house and travel to a place of employment, taking orders and be subject to superiors demands for productivity and accountability.

The fact is that life is in many ways controlled by government agencies and government policies even to the point of discouraging the will to seek employment due to the restrictions of the amount of salary allowable under the assistance guidelines, a factor in the 2008 election, pointed out by a presidential nominee, half of the electorate on government assistance will not vote for him anyway because of his wealth and fear of losing their generous benefits. And true to form, he lost to the nominee who belonged to the party who would most likely increase their benefits resulting in the burden to the employed increased significantly. And the 2016 election brought to the office a shrewd businessman who coined the campaign slogan "Make America Great Again," and against all odds, got swept into office. This resulted in great division, smear campaigns, and the accusations that some foreign power interfered—it had to be, because how was it possible? This whole collusion theory has paralyzed the governing bodies in the capitol, and we the people are poorer for it.

I would even venture to say it has resulted in a poisoned atmosphere and division among the population that will linger long into the next decade.

Question remains, who was served?

Whether we are Republicans or Democrats or not affiliated at all, everyone suffers from the paralysis that is now evident in the houses of Congress and the judiciary. In all this, only one thing is sure: as the influence of the political powers increases, the spiritual powers are diminished. It's as Jesus pointed out: Jesus taught that no one can serve two masters. Matthew 6:24 (KJV) says, "No man can serve two masters: for either he will hate the one and love the other; or else he will hold to the one and despise the other. Ye cannot serve God and mammon."

As the world is ruled by "mammon," or in the modern language "money," and it does take money to purchase the necessities of life, it is easy to see whom we bow down to and whom we serve, and which deity takes priority. This may in large part explain the dwindling numbers of worshippers occupying the pews on any Sunday morning. In many countries in Europe, the cradle-to-grave socialistic government policies are responsible for a 3 percent church attendance. If my earthly life is sustained and depending on the almighty government and not on the Almighty God in heaven, then what can be seen is worshipped more than what is unseen. Well, that necessitates the reorganization of our loyalty and line up our beliefs with the worldly power.

What is starved and neglected is the heart, soul, and mind and the moral state of our being and existence.

Matthew 10:28 says, "And do not fear those who kill the body but cannot kill the soul." The soul is outside the control of the reigning powers. Yes, outside powers can kill the body, but a person still has the power over who he or she will sell the soul to, and when the powers of the world collapse, then who will we turn to?

I remember the time after the Second World War when people flooded churches, maybe not for purely religious reasons but more out of desperation, and as soon as stability and resources reappeared, the need for spiritual sustenance regressed and now it is in a state of irrelevance in the lives of many people as the statistics reveal a very low church attendance in Germany.

The importance of what the Lord Jesus has taught comes to mind in the story of the coin, when the Pharisees tried to entrap the Lord in the relationship of who we pay obedience to (Matthew 22:17–22). "Give to Caesar the things that are Caesar's. And give to God is God's." This tells us that there needs to be a balance. If someone becomes so heavenly that he or she is no earthly good, then that also presents a problem and is not compatible with the Gospel.

Being completely beholden to the earthly powers will set us up for a whole other set of problems as there are no perfect governing authorities, and their damaging policies can turn the world upside down for the average family trying desperately to survive, without a strong faith, where do we find the strength to cope with the dark valleys that David was talking about in Psalm 23? Yes, difficulties *will* come. Know that no matter how difficult it is, we are not alone; my God is with me and he will protect me and lead me beside quiet waters. Without this belief in the promises of God, in many cases, we just simply give up or become so depressed. Many seek refuge in drugs and alcohol to soothe or drown out their fears or anger and make our present circumstances even more difficult.

History has ample proof that people of all nations have risen above their present circumstances and rebuilt their lives and their nations. As an example, to name just a few, Germany, Britain, and the US after WWII and before that, the Civil War and the Great Depression. The Soviet Union and the Communist Bloc nations have failed miserably to recover from WWII. They were not able to provide enough food for their people, and in many years of failed crops, had to turn to the Christian west for grain shipments.

I have observed in my visitations in prisons, hospitals, old age homes, and even mental institutions the differences between people who are relying on their faith in God are better at recovering and leaving the hospital sooner than those where faith is absent. The sheer fact of life is this: Tragedy in life is unavoidable, but misery is a choice. When the first martyr, Stephen, was stoned to death in the Book of Acts 7:59–60: "And as they were stoning Stephen, he called out, 'Lord Jesus, receive my spirit.' And falling to his knees he cried out with a loud voice, 'Lord, do not hold this sin against them.' And when he had said this, he fell asleep."

The world can be and always will be a cruel place. Lord Acton, a British politician, wrote the proverbial saying "Power corrupts; absolute power corrupts absolutely," and it conveys the opinion that as a person's power increases, their moral sense diminishes.

A generation that puts all their trust in the powers of this world—Congress, Senate, courts, or the power of self, believing *I am the master of my life and I decide what I can and do not want to do*—will sooner or later experience the limits of their powers and realize that God and the Word of God is the only thing in this world that does not fluctuate or change direction as the wind blows.

Eve was told by the evil one, "You can be God if you follow my instructions," and she followed him. If we disregard the natural laws instituted by God, we will, as is the case in recent years, call evil good and good evil, and persecute and prosecute people who disagree with the popular will that is sanctified by the highest courts of the land. If God did not create human beings, then they are the evolutionary product of some primordial soup, evolving from our animal forefathers, a monkey.

No-fault divorce may very well have been the capstone that was removed from the foundation. It was the cornerstone of the family, and the family has been in decline ever since ignoring God's degrees. Babies who were conceived by uninhibited sexual desires called free love are aborted. The marriage between people of the same sex, with the proclamation that "love makes a family" and any combination of a group of people cohabiting and copulating with whoever is willing is permitted by law and is socially acceptable. If anyone raises questions about the consequences, they are to be brought to heel with boycotting their livelihoods as in the case of Chick-Fil-A, or any writer or TV host that has any doubts about its validity, colliding with their First Amendment guarantee of freedom of religion and the freedom of speech. They are ostracized and prevented from being promoted in their place of employment or nominated to any political office or survive any congressional hearings.

This is almost an Orwellian prediction coming to pass. "Orwellian" is an adjective describing a situation, idea, or societal condition that George Orwell identified as being destructive to the welfare of a free and open society. It denotes an attitude and a brutal policy of draconian control by propaganda, surveillance, misinformation, denial of truth, and manipulation of the past, including the "unperson"—a person whose past existence is expunged from the public record and memory, practiced by modern repressive governments. Often, this includes the circumstances depicted in his novels, particularly *1984*, where political doublespeak is criticized throughout his work, such as in politics and the English language.

Question: How is it possible that a whole generation, many of them college graduates, indoctrinated by their professors, whose main function is the brainwashing of children to their agenda of a global community? In a global community, all people can extract resources from people of different countries and transfer their wealth to the lesser developed countries so that as in socialistic countries all human desires to thrive and be as productive as possible is extinguished, as promulgated by Karl Marx.

Ronald Reagan said, "Socialism only works in two places: heaven, where they don't need it, and hell, where they already have it." It has been proven over and over, and still the elite educational crowd does not see that the very wealth that allows them to be so intrinsically naïve is a sure prescription for a repeat of the Soviet and Chinese experiments that were and still are a total disaster for the masses, where the very elite that once propagated this system and later came to question the validity are either eliminated or sent to labor camps. And now the Venezuelan experiment, a repeat of a failed system that has brought hardship and loss of freedom and impediment to the human spirit of entrepreneurship and commerce, destroying one of the wealthiest economies in the southern hemisphere of the Americas.

Violent protests and upheavals in the streets may not be the answer to this regime, as it was in East Germany and China, in 1973 and 1989 respectively; and Czechoslovakia in 1968 and Hungary in 1956. Mahatma Gandhi, a student of the New Testament, which he carried a copy with him all times, resorted to nonviolent protest to accomplish the impossible, the removal of the British Empire in 1949 from the Indian continent. Zacharias 4:6 reads, "Not by power nor by might, but only by the spirit of the Lord." Psalm 20:7 says, "Some trust in chariots, and some in horses, but we trust the name of Yahweh our God."

In America today, there seems to be the belief that more military might and power will secure the world domination of American influence at the cost of one third of the economic wealth on military hardware financed with borrowed money from abroad. This heavy debt load is incurred by the belief that "Might Makes Right," and it comes at a heavy cost to especially the millennial generation, as they are approaching the so-called golden years, and their children, who will be at the mercy of foreign lenders. The Bible does not prohibit debt; however, everywhere that debt is mentioned, it is discussed in a negative light. The main reason for this is it makes you a servant to someone other than God.

Proverbs 22:7 says, "The rich rule over the poor, and the borrower is servant to the lender." There are already countries like China who own 1.6 trillion US treasury bonds, which need to be repaid when they mature. Therefore, they have a tremendous influence on the ability of the US government to finance their budget deficits and even to defend themselves. Whether somebody believes or disbelieves what the Bible says, the truth is the truth, and it will exact a heavy price when ignored.

Question still remains: in whom does one put their trust in? The rulers who have diluted the savings of the hardworking people earned through their working years? Joshua told his people, "As for me and my house, we trust in the Lord." Faith in God is, and always will be, a necessary ingredient in people's life to continue in their pursuit of their dreams and aspirations through all the difficulties and bumps in the road they may encounter. If the millennial generation continues in their quest to either shun or even belittle those who are leaning on the everlasting arms of the Lord, and instead lean and trust in their present leaders, they are in danger of losing all hope and reach for some relief in whatever may be available to lull them into a temporary numbness from their troubles.

This may be the explanation for the explosion of the number of opioid overdoses besetting our country. Seventy thousand per year are overdosing, and that's not even counting the numbers of those being severely impacted and unable to lead a productive life and being a statistic of the government assistance culture. I am not a particularly overly religious person, but my life experience has taught me to follow a teaching that provided me with a life worth living.

In my most desperate moments of life, I turned to the Lord for strength and healing and found the peace that surpasses all human understanding. There was no longing for alcohol or drugs; I sought and found the strength and the power to overcome in the nourishment that I received in the Eucharist and in my faith. I knew that I was now not alone, and that my God would lead me to greener pastures and quiet waters, and he did!

Many conclude there are other ways and methods to a peaceful life. Hindu and Buddhist teachings and meditations are wonderful ways for relaxation, but when we consider the general population in the countries where it is the dominant religion, it did not result in a life that even remotely resembles the average way of life Christians take for granted in the Christian west, and have remained in the throes of a third world standard of living for the masses, and that has not changed even to this day.

Chapter 24

Economic Impoverishment through the Exportation of Employment Opportunities to Third World Countries

The loss of millions of blue-collar jobs due to the transfer of factories and technology to third-world countries with little or no worker protections, environmental safeguards and pay scales that have not even approached the level of early nineteen century working conditions in western societies, has seriously deteriorated the purchasing power of the average family, especially in inner-American cities, forcing half the population to rely either on unemployment and more complete government handouts for their subsistence.

This is especially true with the high level of youth unemployment, which is in the 20 to 30 percent range in formerly very industrious cities across the US. Sidney, Nebraska, with a population of 6,300 is a good example of how venture capitalists have been able to destroy rural American towns. Cabela's was the major employer until a venture capitalist bought a block of shares in the company and forced a sale of the company to Bass-Pro, of which he was the majority stockholder. He then sold of all the assets and moved production overseas and left the town of Sydney devastated with a loss of 2,000 jobs.

This scenario of unscrupulous venture capitalists has been allowed to devastate countless cities and towns all over America, reminiscent of the robber barons of the early nineteenth century, with the likes of Jacob Astor, John D. Rockefeller, and Andrew Carnegie, but to my knowledge they did not yet transfer entire industries and jobs overseas. A chief complaint against the nineteenth-century capitalists was that they were monopolists. Fear over the robber barons and their monopoly practices increased public support for the Sherman Antitrust Act of 1890.

Economic theory says a monopolist earns premium profits by restricting output and raising prices. This only occurs after the monopolist prices out or legally restricts any competitor firms in the industry. However, there is no historical evidence that natural monopolies formed before the Sherman Antitrust Act. Many so-called robber barons—James J. Hill, Henry Ford, Andrew Carnegie, Cornelius Vanderbilt, and John D. Rockefeller—became wealthy entrepreneurs through product innovation and business efficiency. Of the goods and services they provided, supply grew, and prices fell rapidly, greatly boosting Americans' standards of living. This is the opposite of monopolistic behavior.

Other common criticisms of the early robber barons included poor working conditions for employees, selfishness, and greed. The rise of labor unions and government laws have alleviated many of these poor working conditions. Working conditions in nineteenth century America were often challenging, but workers may have been better off working for a robber baron. Rockefeller and Ford, for example, paid higher-than-average wages, including bonuses for innovation or exceptional production.

Working conditions were very harsh in many industries, but jobs remained in the land, compared to what has happened under the global economy model of shutting down, dismantling and moving production overseas where child labor and poor working conditions are still allowed. Outsourcing jobs overseas has added millions of people on to the unemployment and welfare rolls and diminished their ability to purchase the same products the workers used to produce right here in their hometowns in the USA.

European countries have for the most part prohibited this practice by Wall Street corporate raiders as it was destroying European workers ability to earn a living in their communities. Corporations who are controlled and managed by unscrupulous CEOs and CFOs without ethics or moral obligations and responsibilities toward the welfare of their employees and their communities have devastated millions of lives.

Millennials who have abandoned the faith of their parents and exchanged it for a secular worldview that is opposed to a Christian worldview may not fully realize what impact a world without biblical values entails and are fallible and likely to follow like sheep to the slaughter, or, like in the legend of the Pied Piper of Hamelin, are led to drowning in debt and inability to deal with their circumstances and the stress it entails.

Chapter 25

Christian Morals and Values

Chuck Colson wrote in 1999, "Now how shall we live?" And that is the question: How will the generation born between 1980–2010 live in this post-modern world? As Chuck Colson puts it, "We live in a culture that is at best morally indifferent...in which Judeo-Christian values are mocked...in which violence, banality, meanness, and disintegrating personal behavior are destroying civility and endangering the very life of our communities." Is this the kind of world we want our children and their children's children to live in?

Question: How can this falling away from the faith of their parents improve their situation? First Peter 5:8–9 says, "Be alert and of sober mind. Your enemy the devil prowls around like a roaring lion looking for someone to devour. Resist him, standing firm in the faith, because you know that the family of believers throughout the world is undergoing the same kind of sufferings."

There are many demonic imposters, may they be politicians or demagogues who recruit people to commit acts of civil disobedience. They host demonstrations that frequently turn violent, and when questioned why they are demonstrating, cannot produce a valid reason or purpose.

Sadly, many demonstrators are the products of hardworking families, many, who have never themselves had the opportunity to go to college, and with much sweat, worked two jobs to afford and make it possible for their children to be educated and then find out that their children are being brainwashed by extreme liberal college culture professors and administrators who then use them for their left-leaning political agenda, a stark reminder of how the Third Reich Hitler used the youth.

What is at hand here in the US is the systematic attempt for complete removal of the Christian values and faith from the public square. The establishment is very aware of the words Jesus spoke: "I am the way, the truth and the life, and the truth will set you free." Or like Dr. Martin Luther King spoke from the mall in Washington, "Free at last, free at last." He knew that a racist cannot reconcile his faith in Jesus and deny people of color their God-given right for equal rights.

The Christian worldview and a culture of unnatural lifestyles and death cannot coexist side by side; consequently, one needs to be eliminated or marginalized, as the Lord said, "No one can serve two masters. For you will hate one and love the other; you will be devoted to one and despise the other. You cannot serve God and mammon (money)" (Matthew 6:24).

The love of money, meaning more opportunities for the white population was the driving motivation for the segregation of the races, they must have known in their hearts that that is in direct opposition to the teachings of Jesus. Dr. King knew this too, for this reason he appealed to the moral obligation of the white population, which by the way, in those days, attended church in much larger numbers. The story is told that just because people are attending Christian church does not make them necessarily a Christian, just as if someone sitting faithfully in their garage on Sunday mornings does not make them a Mercedes. So a megachurch with elaborate lighting and professional musicians and a great orator will not encourage or produce the kind of worshipper that our Lord Jesus had in mind for his kingdom of God.

The Lord was speaking with the woman at the well when she asked Jesus where she must worship.

> "Sir," the woman said, "I can see that you are a prophet. Our ancestors worshiped on this mountain, but you Jews claim that the place where we must worship is in Jerusalem."

> "Woman," Jesus replied, "believe me, a time is coming when you will worship the Father neither on this mountain nor in Jerusalem. You Samaritans worship what you do not know; we worship what we do know, for salvation is from the Jews. Yet a time is coming and has now come when the true worshipers will worship the Father in the Spirit and in truth, for they are the kind of worshipers the Father seeks. God is spirit, and his worshipers must worship in the Spirit and in truth." (John 4:19–24)

This passage and the discourse between Jesus and the woman about where and what kind of worshipping the Lord expects from his followers shows clearly the direction the Lord had in mind. Directly relating to the passage in John 2:19 where Jesus answered them, "Destroy this temple, and I will raise it again in three days," Jesus was referring to the resurrection and a new kind of worshipper. The people around him did not grasp what was the meaning of this. Reading the Book of Acts reveals the disciples' actions as they went out and spread the Good News! The power of the Good News has not weakened or changed, only the church has changed as it has assimilated and attached itself to the power of the prevailing cultural moors and subverted the body of Christ. The Roman Catholic Church with its worldwide institutions and power has used its power to gain and enrich the Church. The Reformation divided the church and has produced according to the Center for the Study of Global Christianity (CSGC) at Gordon-Conwell Theological Seminary, approximately 41,000 Christian denominations in the world today.

What could be more confusing to a child or a young adult more than to choose from 1,000 different traditions and interpretations of the Gospel? Jesus taught that a divided house cannot stand, and we are experiencing a catastrophic decline in churches worldwide, and not because the Gospel has weakened but the worshippers have abandoned the Gospel truth. Young people are still young people with eyes to see and ears to hear, and through the advancement of technological empowerment of knowledge available to them, it is not hard to understand why they question the wisdom of the church hierarchy and the perversion of the use of the tithings that are collected by the millions, with much of it used for the enjoyment of the ministers rather than to alleviate the suffering of the poor. The present situation of the young who are not participating in church life may be a silver lining, and in a way forcing the change needed to advance the Gospel in these modern times.

Authenticity will always win over inauthenticity, giving credence to the words of Jesus, "I am the way and the truth." The truth has not changed, only the interpretations have changed. We are now able, with new technology, to have every kind of translation in existence at our fingertips on our computers. We can use the one we, the worshipper, might like the most.

Not to exonerate the Catholic Church in any way, but it is still the one church who adheres more to the Gospel and the traditions of the early church. Tradition does not replace the Gospel, but traditions have been the way people worshipped from the beginning, in the Old Testament and the New Testament. The way they worship follows the traditions they observed for many generations. What Sunday of the month Holy Communion is observed, what Scripture, or when the Lord's Prayer is prayed at what time during worship service?

In the Congregational Church I attend, just a few years back, women could not serve as deacons, and later, when women could serve, they could only wear skirts and not pants. The myriad of denominations all serve a purpose, and that purpose should always be the equipping and mentoring of the congregants to be communicators of the Gospel. Some are born evangelists, others are struggling, but the original evangelists where all amateurs, and it was the Holy Spirit that gave them the courage and the words. Luke 12:11 tells us, "When you are brought before synagogues, rulers and authorities, do not worry about how you will defend yourselves or what you will say, for the Holy Spirit will teach you at that time what you should say."

This will be of utmost importance for the future of Christianity, believers are intimidated by the postmodern popular culture into keeping their faith in Christ in their church and in private, and especially not share their faith at places of employment. The popular wisdom: never talk about politics and religion when you are in company—well, those should be the places to share our faith and what we believe and why we believe. If faith has strengthened us and has helped us overcome adversity in our life, then why do we not share our faith?

There must be a strong sense of conviction when talking about the Gospel. A good example is the apostle Paul. He was beaten many times for his convictions and once even left for dead, but he later wrote: "I know whom I have believed, and I am persuaded, I finished the race and fought the good fight." It is that kind of conviction that needs to be displayed.

The mark of a successful salesmen is the conviction that the product he is selling will benefit his customers and that they cannot possibly be without that product. The salesman needs to persevere in his mission to bring the best product to his customers. The early Christians did exactly that; they even made the people aware of the heavenly benefits and eternal life. In our present world today there needs to be that kind of zeal and resurgence to proclaim the Gospel not only in church on Sunday morning but in everyday activities, wherever people gather or congregate.

Someone made the comment, "The most dangerous place to be on a Sunday morning is a church parking lot after the Mass or service is out." Worshippers did their prescribed duty to attend Mass or services, but as soon as the last word of the benediction is spoken, head for the exit doors and leave behind what they just heard and go on with their plans for the day.

Children take their cues from their parents, who made them come to church, but their complacency about sharing their faith and not defending it is really telling their children it can't be that important, and as soon as they have pleased their parents by going through the confirmation process and are preparing for college, they leave their faith and practices of the faith behind, like a garment that just does not look right in their places of learning and that doesn't fit in anymore in this New Age culture.

What is very interesting is the fact that many of the young in the US are falling away from the faith of their parents and fall prey to socialistic orators, who find very fertile ground and gain many followers.

So, what will the new garments look like when it is adorning their bodies? Is it made of quality cloth? Or is the fabric flimsy enough that one can see right through it, of such poor quality that it will disintegrate quickly when on their journey of life?

"The garment of praise," to quote from the KJV Bible. To appoint unto them that mourn in Zion, to give unto them beauty for ashes, the oil of joy for mourning, the garment of praise for the spirit of heaviness; that they might be called trees of righteousness, the planting of the Lord, that he might be glorified. Isaiah 61:3

Would there be any indication that the Lord might or will be glorified?

If we deny his existence, why would anyone want to glorify God? History has proven over and over, where God is not praised as Lord of all, there will be worshipping of an alternative god instead of the God of the Bible. And in whatever form it may be, anyone with charisma and the promise of a new just society—communism and socialism, as an example—once the new leaders were able to eliminate enough opposition and gained absolute power, that power corrupted absolutely.

It is estimated that 200 million people perished in the socialistic experiment in countries that were and are still ruled by socialist governments. In the People's Republic of China, to this day, they have Gulag Camps, reminiscent of the Stalin-era internment camps in Siberia where Muslims, Christians, writers, journalists, or anyone opposing the dictatorial system of government were sent to, what they call now, reeducation camps.

The Gulag Archipelago was written by the Russian author Alexander Solzhenitsyn, who survived the Gulag. During his incarceration, he was able to spirit a copy to the west, exposing the horrendous circumstances that exist in the "People's Paradise" called the Soviet Union. You must understand, the leading Bolsheviks who took over Russia were not Russians. They hated Russians. They hated

Christians. Driven by ethnic hatred, they tortured and slaughtered millions of Russians without a shred of human remorse. And that cannot be overstated enough. Bolshevism committed the greatest human slaughter of all time. The fact that most of the world is ignorant and uncaring about this enormous crime is proof that the global media is in the hands of the perpetrators.

The Gulag system declined after the death of Joseph Stalin, and prisoners were slowly being released, starting in 1954. The Gulag program was officially ended with a government decree in 1960. The collapse of the Soviet Union in 1990 has brought the Russian faith community back to the forefront of life in Russia as churches and seminaries have been reestablished and are flourishing. All is not yet well as the old guard is still subverting the democratic institutions with very questionable practices.

The American media is on a warpath against Christianity because it presents a roadblock for the New Age/New worldview and way of life that cannot be reconciled with a biblical worldview of moral and ethical boundaries that are the foundation of a democratic society. It is this truth that needs to be excised from public life. Alexander Solzhenitsyn wrote in *The Gulag Archipelago*:

> The strength or weakness of a society depends more on the level of its spiritual life than on its level of industrialization. Neither a market economy nor even general abundance constitutes the crowning achievement of human life. If a nation's spiritual energies have been exhausted, it will not be saved from collapse by the most perfect government structure or by any industrial development. A tree with a rotten core cannot stand. We hear a constant clamor for rights, rights, always rights, but so very little about responsibility. And we have forgotten God. The need now is for selflessness, for a spirit of sacrifice, for a willingness to put aside personal gains for the salvation of the whole Western world.

As Pope Benedict XVI points out in "Spe Salvi" (English: "Saved in Hope"), referencing the Latin phrase from Romans 8:24, "Spesalvi facti sumus" ("in hope we were saved"), is the second encyclical letter promulgated on November 30, 2007, and is about the theological virtue of hope. A society that rejects Christ does not simply move on. Rather, this kind of society, echoing Kant, must be in opposition to Christ. So instead of post-Christian, a society that has rejected Christianity, must necessarily become anti-Christian: "There is no doubt, therefore, that a 'Kingdom of God' accomplished without God—a kingdom therefore of man alone—inevitably ends up as the 'perverse end' of all things," as described by Kant [reign of the Anti-Christ]: "we have seen it, and we see it over and over again." Where strange symbols and new ideologies replace the Cross, those who live by the Cross cannot be tolerated. Immanuel Kant was a German philosopher in the Age of Enlightenment. In his doctrine of transcendental idealism, he argued that space, time, and causation are mere sensibilities; "things-in-themselves" exist, but their nature is unknowable. In his view, the mind shapes and structures experience, with all human experience sharing certain structural features. Kant believed that reason is the source of morality, and that aesthetics arise from a faculty of disinterested judgment. Kant's views continue to have a major influence on contemporary philosophy, especially the fields of ethics, political theory, and postmodern aesthetics.

As Cardinal Joseph Ratzinger explained, "Meanwhile, the fact remains that this democracy [modern] is a product of the fusion of the Greek and the Christian heritage and therefore can survive only in this foundational connection. If we do not recognize this again and accordingly learn to live democracy with a view to Christianity and Christianity with a view to the free democratic state, we will surely gamble away democracy."

John Winthrop's sermon to the settlers said, "We shall find that the God of Israel is among us, when ten of us shall be able to resist a thousand of our enemies; when he shall make us a praise and a glory, that men shall say of succeeding plantations, 'The Lord make it like that of New England.' For we must consider that we shall be as a City upon a hill." Recall that John Winthrop added a warning that our politicians typically fail to mention, but that echoes in Pope Benedict XVI's warnings: "The eyes of all people are upon us. So that if we shall deal falsely with our God in this work we have undertaken, and so cause him to withdraw his present help from us, we shall be made a story and a by-word throughout the world."

Chapter 26

One Nation under God

The United States, a republic of fifty states, governed by Three Branches of Government of checks and balances, has allowed this republic to prosper beyond the wildest imaginations of the original writers of the US Constitution.

A quote from Ronald Reagan about our nation follows that "<u>If</u> we ever forget that we're one nation under God, then we will be a nation gone under." There are serious efforts in Congress to eliminate "One Nation Under God" from the pledge of allegiance. Then the question arises, who will this United States be *under?*

This is a reminder that we will have this republic—"Under God"—only for as long as we keep it under God. Isaiah gives a sobering warning what will be in store when a nation is not one nation under God!

Isaiah 61:3 (KJV) says, "To appoint unto them that mourn in Zion, to give unto them beauty for ashes, the oil of joy for mourning, the garment of praise for the spirit of heaviness; that they might be called trees of righteousness, the planting of the Lord, that he might be glorified."

Who will the new garment represent?

Who decides what kind of garment we will be required to wear and what color will it be? And who is getting all the praise? Who and what will be worshipped?

NOTES

Chapter 3

Pg. 18. James Macintyre, Christian Today, "Germany: Steep decline in Catholic church attendance," 18 July 2016, Limburg Bishop Georg Batzing who spoke during a March 3, 2020, news conference.

Pg. 30· Saint Augustine of Hippo, Confessions, is an autobiographical work consisting of 13 books written in Latin between AD 397 and 400.

Chapter 7

Pg. 43. John Cornwell, Hitler's Pope: The Secret History of Pius XII, Penguin Books, October 26th 2000, (first published August 28th 1999).

Pg. 44. Martin Niemöller, The Holocaust Encyclopedia, https://encyclopedia.ushmm.org/content/en/article/martin-niemoeller-biography (1892–1984).

Pg. 47. Michel de Montaigne, "A good marriage would be between a blind wife and a deaf husband," Michel de Montaigne (1533-1592) was one of the most significant philosophers of the French Renaissance.

Chapter 8

Pg. 50. Quran (3:36, 3:151, 4:76, 4:89)

Chapter 9

    Pg. 53. Erwin Lutzer, When a nation forgets God, U.S. Supreme Court, Roe v. Wade, 410 U.S. 113 (1973)

Chapter 11

    Pg. 60. Leo Tolstoy, War and Peace, 1865–1867

Chapter 12

    Pg. 65. Josef H. Darchinger, Wirtschaftswunder, "West Germany amazed the world with its energized ascension to economic powerhouse." Jul 01, 2008.

Chapter 14

    Pg. 69. Aleksandr Solzhenitsyn, The Gulag Archipelago, An Experiment in Literary Investigation, non-fiction text written between 1958 and 1968 by Russian writer and dissident Solzhenitsyn. It was first published in 1973.

Chapter 15

    Pg. 73. Thomas Cahill, How the Irish Saved Civilization: The Untold Story of Ireland's Heroic Role from the Fall of Rome to the Rise of Medieval Europe.

Chapter 16

    Pg. 80. Jake Tapper, CNN interview with Mike Pence: "Ninety percent of the people never show up for their hearing in the months ahead," and "One in five US prison inmates is a 'criminal alien,'" Referring to the July 2018 U.S. Government Accountability Office Report to Congressional Requesters: GAO-18-433 Criminal Alien Statistics: Information on

Incarcerations, Arrests, Convictions, Cost, and Removals, June 23, 2019.

Pg. 87. James Vincent Schall S.J., quoted in BrainyQuotes.com, James V. Schall (January 20, 1928–April 17, 2019) was an American Jesuit Roman Catholic priest, teacher, writer, and philosopher.

Pg. 90. Heather McDonald, The Diversity Delusion, How Race and Gender Pandering Corrupt the University and Undermine Our Culture.

Chapter 17

Pg. 97. Abdelwahab Meddeb, The Malady of Islam, emphasizes the loss of scientific creativity, cultural suppleness, and eros. libertybooks.com.

Pg. 99. Quran (5:51, 5:57, 5:80, 3:118)

Chapter 18

Pg. 101. Federal United States immigration legislation, "The Immigration Act of 1907," passed by the 59th Congress and signed into law by President Theodore Roosevelt on February 20, 1907.

Chapter 19

Pg. 104. Mollie Hemingway, Christine Blasey Ford Attorney Admits Abortion Support 'Motivated' Anti-Kavanaugh Accusations, September 4, 2019.

Chapter 22

Pg. 115. Charles Darwin, On the Origin of Species 1859, Adam M. Goldstein, editor, New York , NY: American Museum of Natural History, 2011. 1 fig., xxxii + 298 pp. 23,

Chapter 22

Pg. 118. Melanie Arter, "New York Gov. Andrew Cuomo Signs Law Legalizing Late-Term Abortion," Obama speaking at a media event in Turkey April 6, 2009 Obama remarked, "I've said before that one of the great strengths of the United States is—although as I mentioned we have a very large Christian population—we do not consider ourselves a Christian nation, or a Jewish nation or a Muslim nation, January 2019.

Chapter 25

Pg. 138. Aleksandr Solzhenitsyn, The Gulag Archipelago, An Experiment in Literary Investigation.

Pg. 139. Benedict XVI, Saved in Hope: Spe Salvi, the Pope's Official Documents of the Roman Catholic Church.

About the Author

Josef Herz has been president and owner of a food-processing company for twenty-seven years and volunteering in Christian ministry for twenty-four years in youth and adult prisons. Upon retiring from business, serving as volunteer chaplain at Masonicare, Middlesex Hospital, and Connecticut Valley Hospital for eight years. Born in Germany in 1943 into a family of ten children, attending schools in Germany before emigrating to the United States with his wife, Roswitha. They have three children, five grandchildren, and four great-grandchildren.

CPSIA information can be obtained
at www.ICGtesting.com
Printed in the USA
LVHW030939171221
706260LV00004B/385